für
Jakob

LONE RACER ©2006 NICOLAS MAHLER

ISBN 978-1-891830-69-3
1. CARTOONS / HUMOR
2. RACING
3. GRAPHIC NOVELS

TOP SHELF PRODUCTIONS
PO BOX 1282
MARIETTA, GA
30061-1282
USA

WWW.TOPSHELFCOMIX.COM

PUBLISHED BY TOP SHELF PRODUCTIONS, INC.
PUBLISHERS: BRETT WARNOCK AND CHRIS STAROS.
PRODUCTION: CHRISTOPHER ROSS.
TRANSLATED BY MARK NEVINS.

FIRST PRINTING, DECEMBER 2006
PRINTED IN CANADA.

NICOLAS MAHLER

LONE RACER

TOP SHELF PRODUCTIONS
ATLANTA / PORTLAND

1

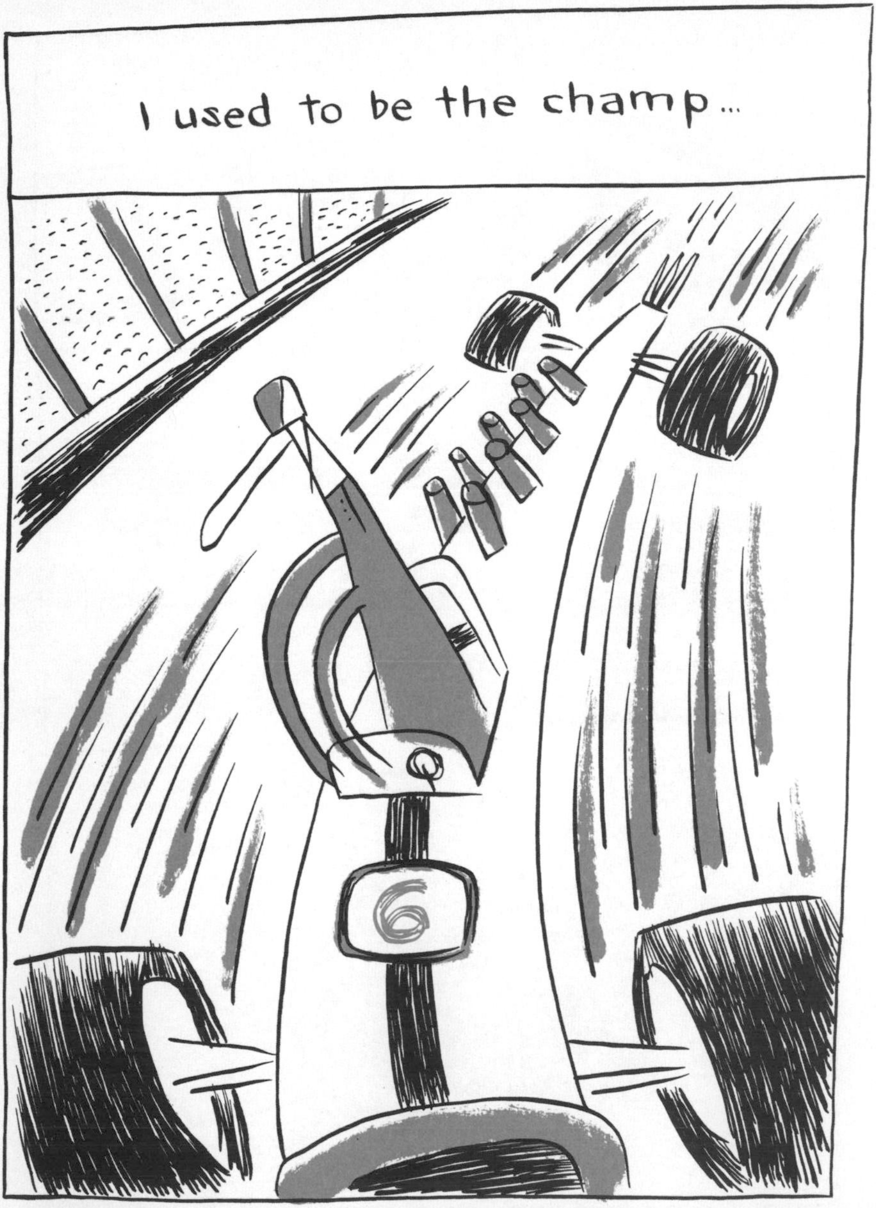
I used to be the champ...
6

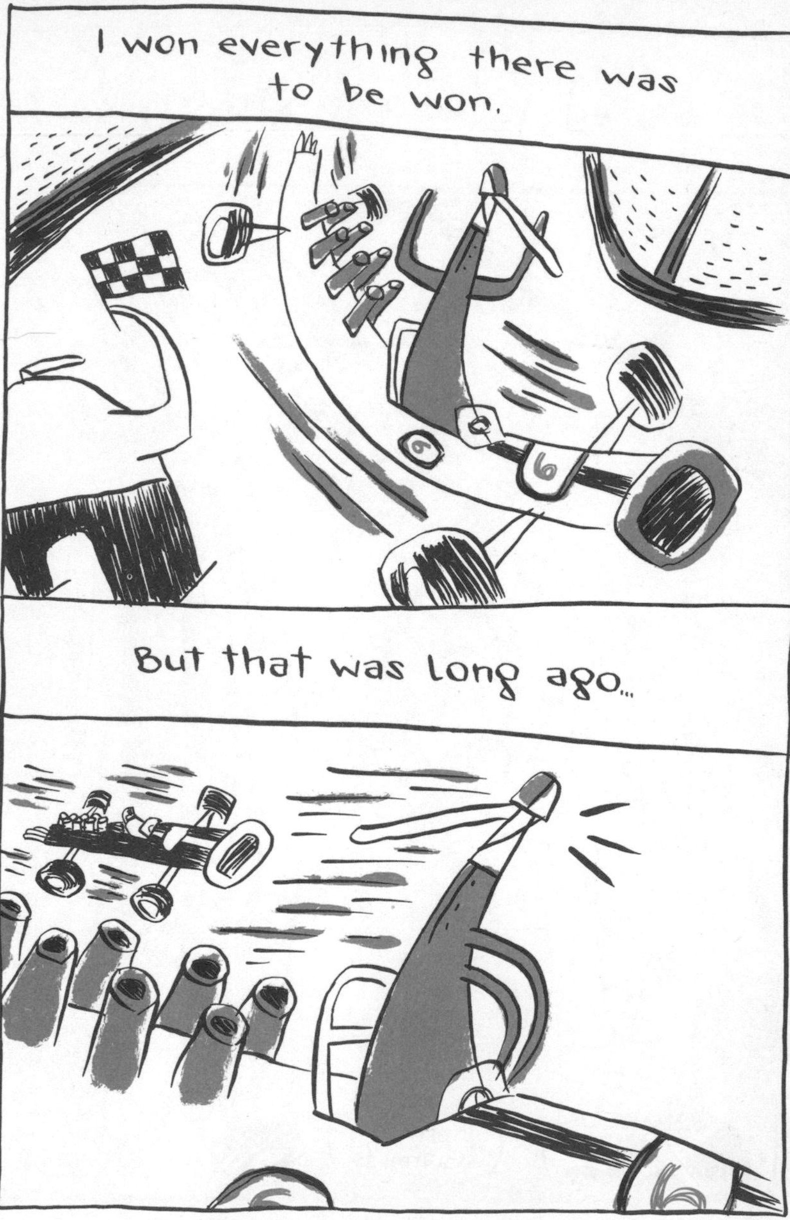
I won everything there was to be won.
But that was long ago...

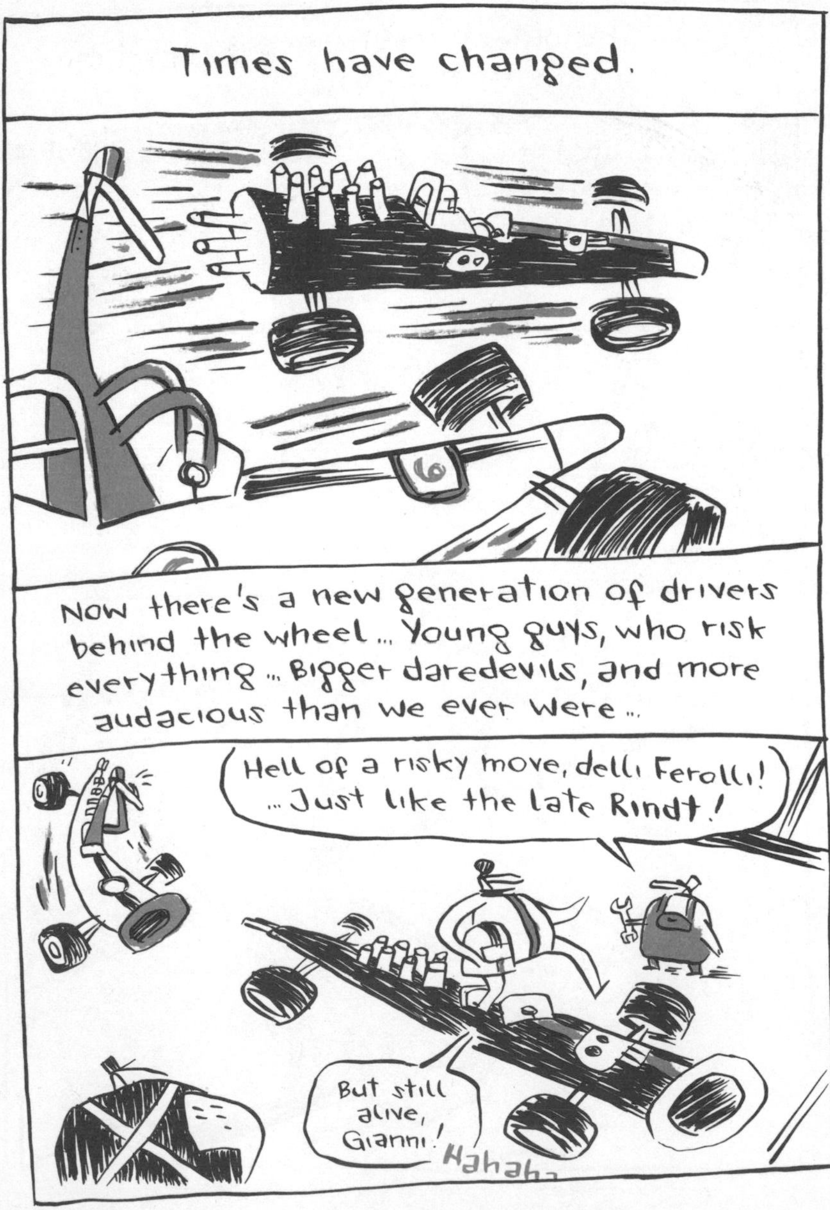

Times have changed.
Now there's a new generation of drivers behind the wheel... Young guys, who risk everything... Bigger daredevils, and more audacious than we ever were...
Hell of a risky move, delli Ferolli! ...Just like the late Rindt!
But still alive, Gianni!
Hahaha

Only the oldest mechanics know, how good I once was ...
My grandfather drives better than that creep ...
Well ... back in the day ... he was... he was big.
I'm still big.

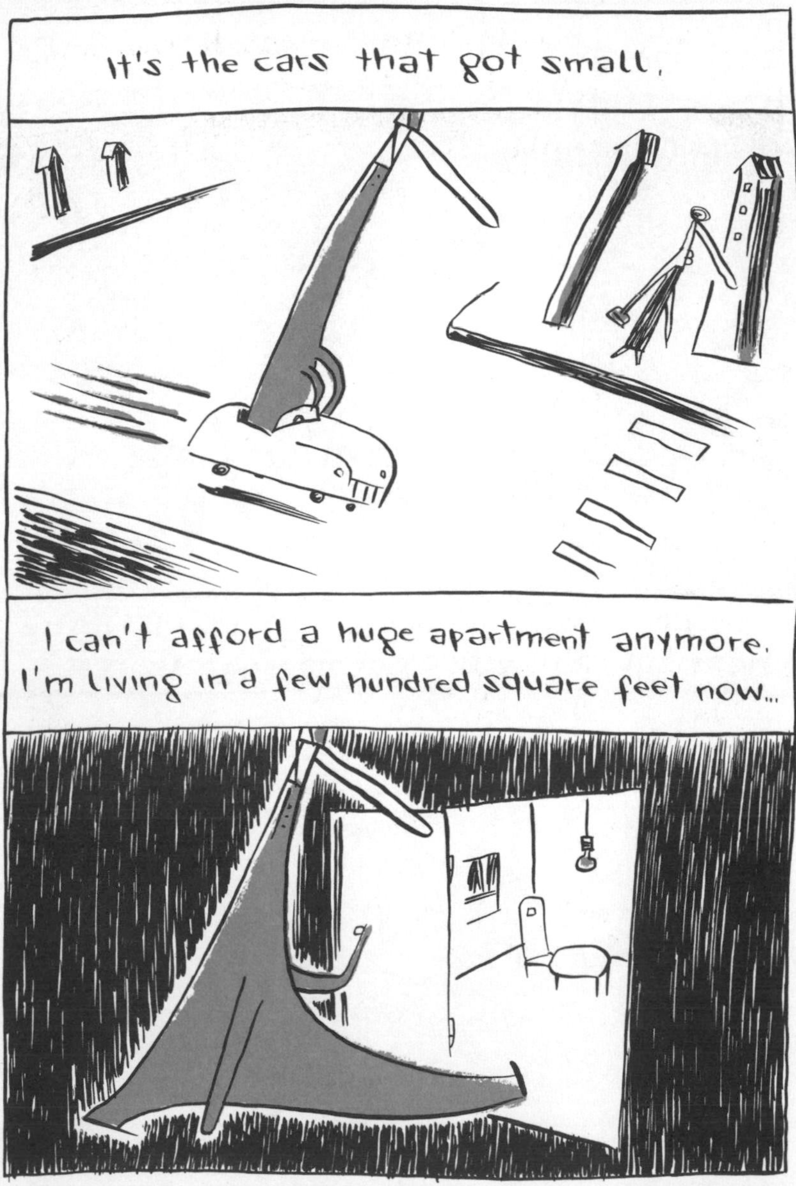
It's the cars that got small.
I can't afford a huge apartment anymore.
I'm living in a few hundred square feet now...

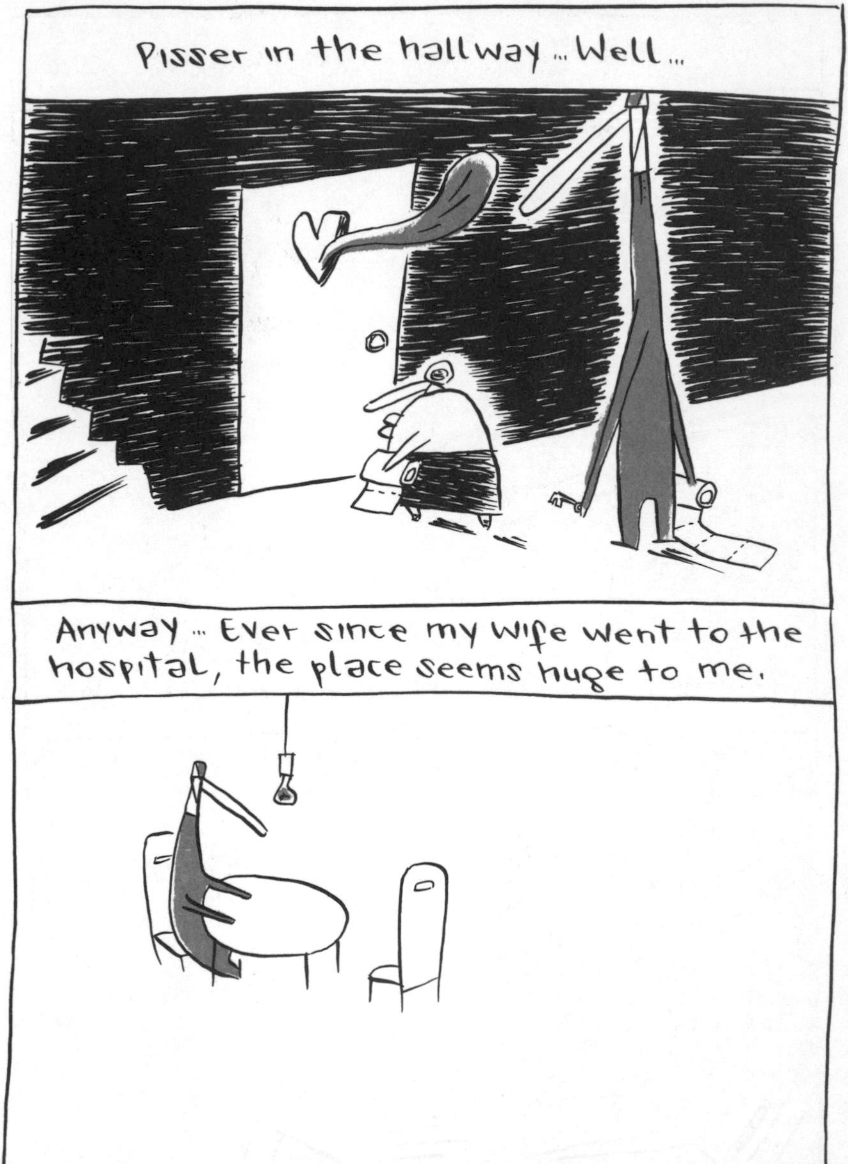
Pisser in the hallway ... Well ...
Anyway ... Ever since my wife went to the hospital, the place seems huge to me.

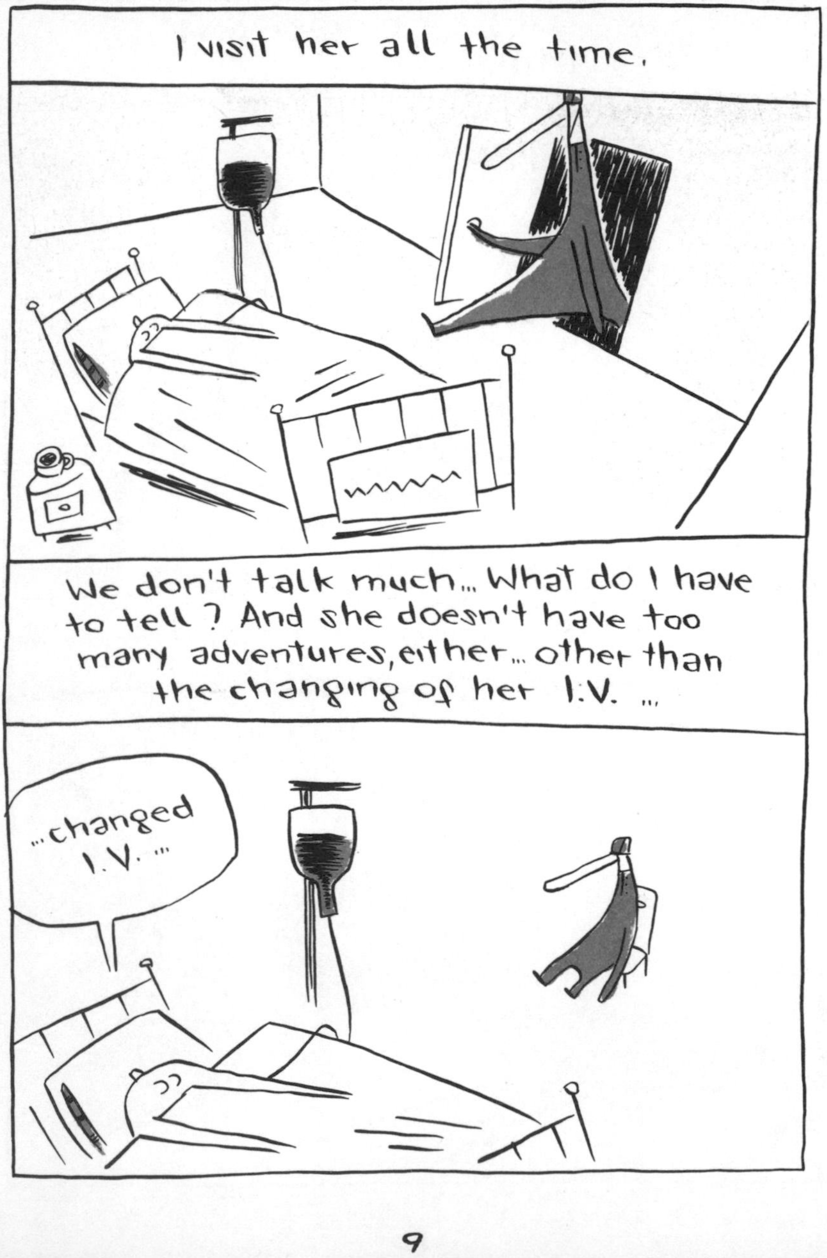
I visit her all the time.
We don't talk much... What do I have to tell? And she doesn't have too many adventures, either... other than the changing of her I.V. ...
...changed I.V. ...

Afterwards, I always feel really crappy.

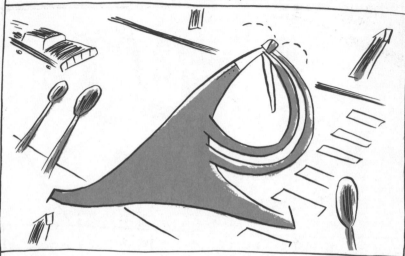

Thank heavens for BAR JUANJO.

There's always someone there who knows me.

"Rubber", for instance, an old racing pal of mine.

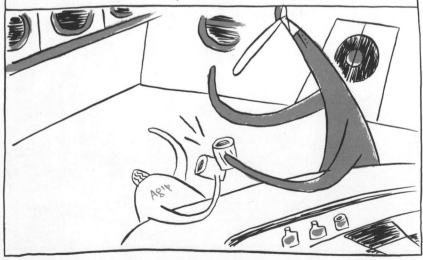

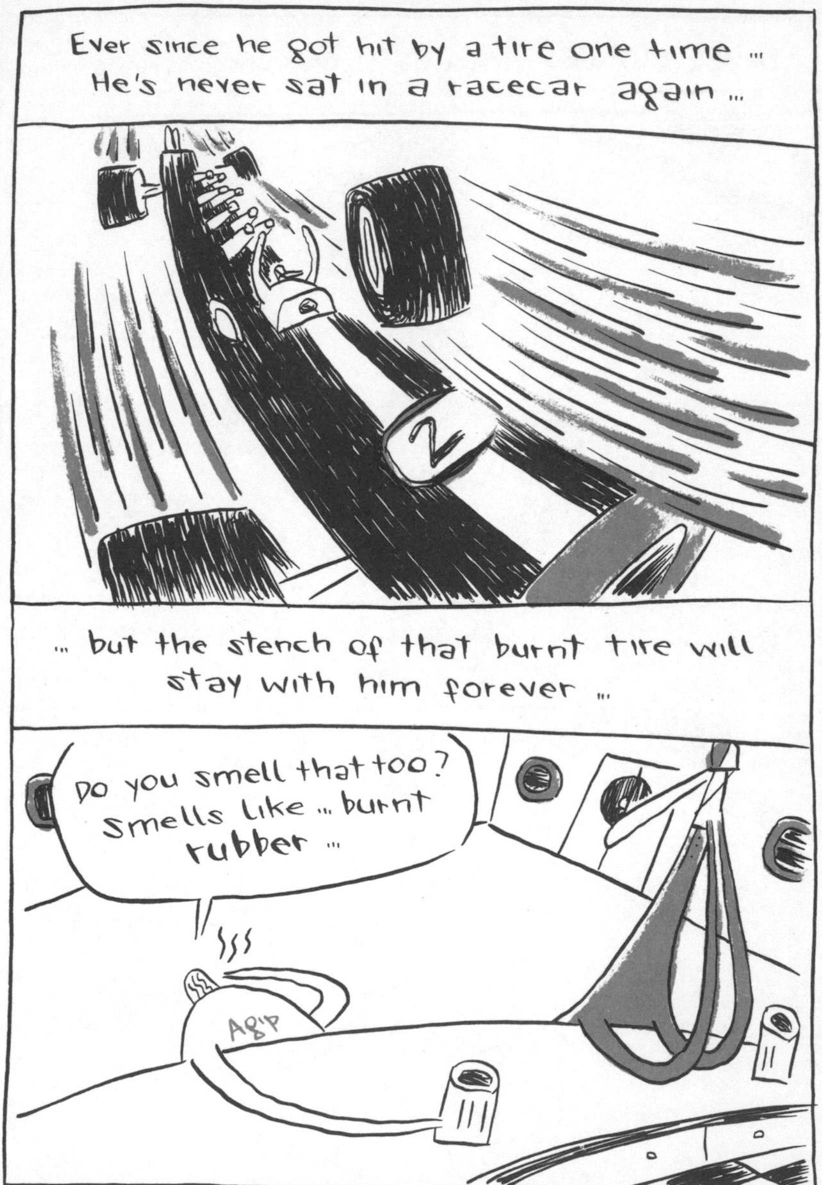
Ever since he got hit by a tire one time ... He's never sat in a racecar again ...
2
... but the stench of that burnt tire will stay with him forever ...
Do you smell that too? Smells like ... burnt rubber ...
Agip

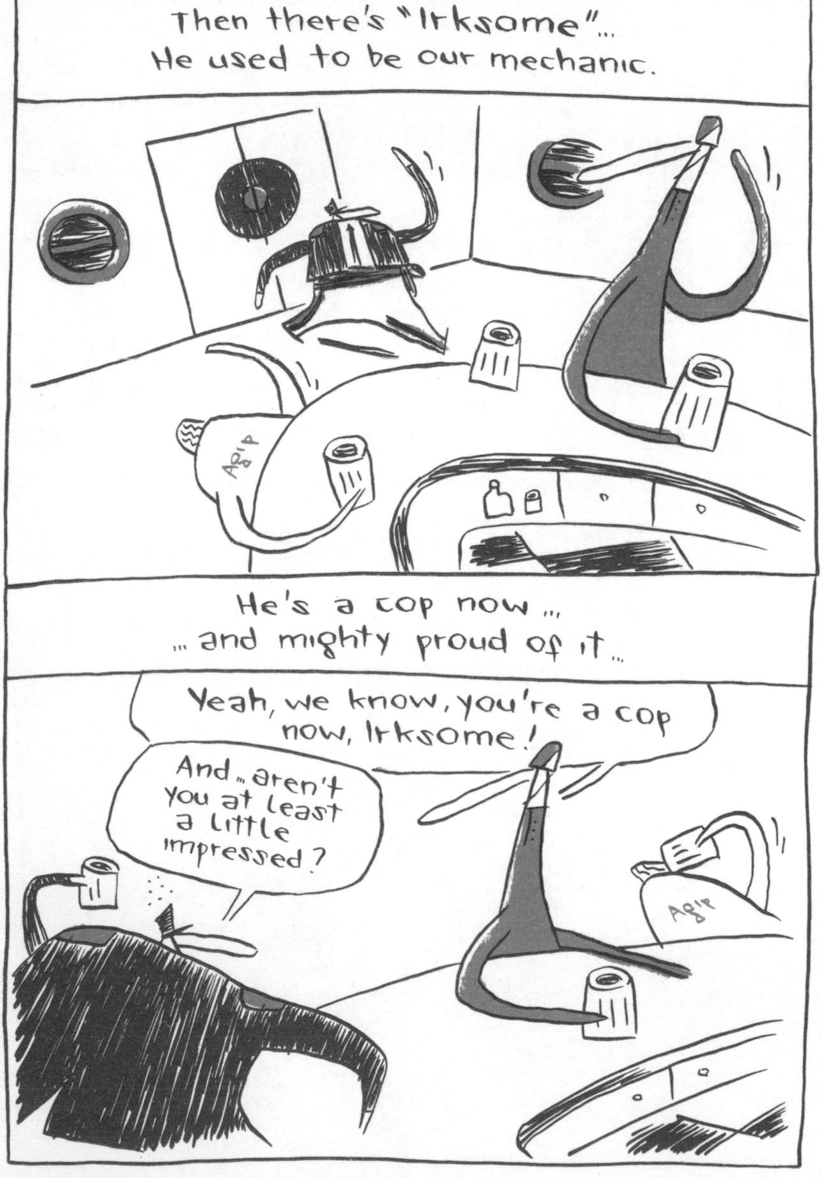

Then there's "Irksome"... He used to be our mechanic.
He's a cop now ... ... and mighty proud of it ...
Yeah, we know, you're a cop now, Irksome!
And ... aren't you at least a little impressed?

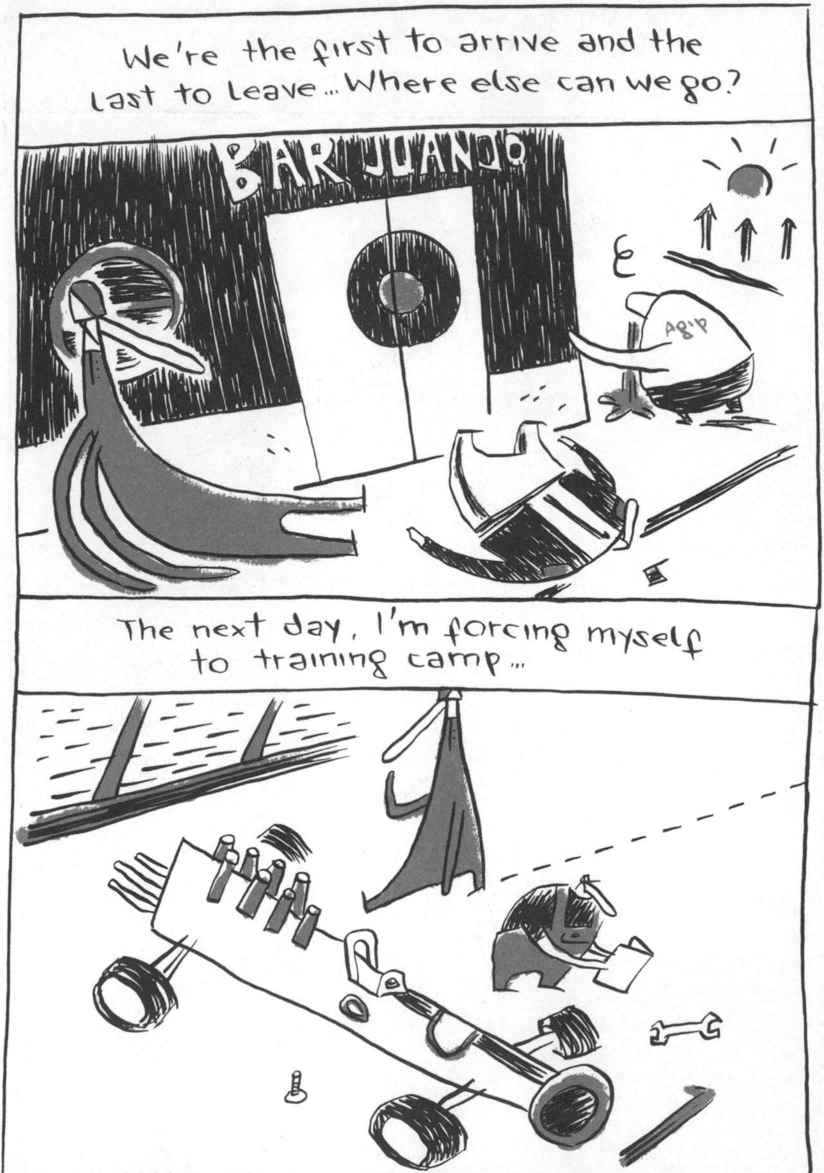
We're the first to arrive and the last to leave... Where else can we go?
BAR JUANDO
Agip
The next day, I'm forcing myself to training camp...

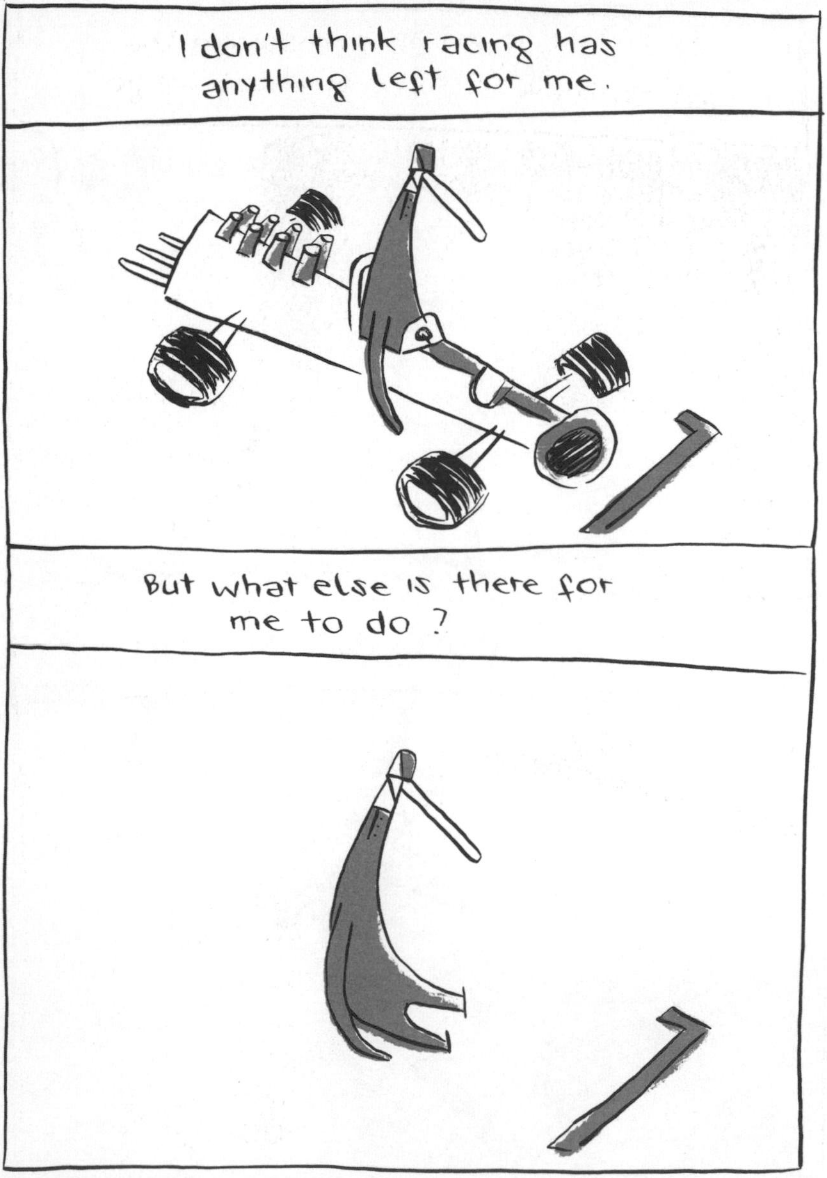
I don't think racing has anything left for me.
But what else is there for me to do?

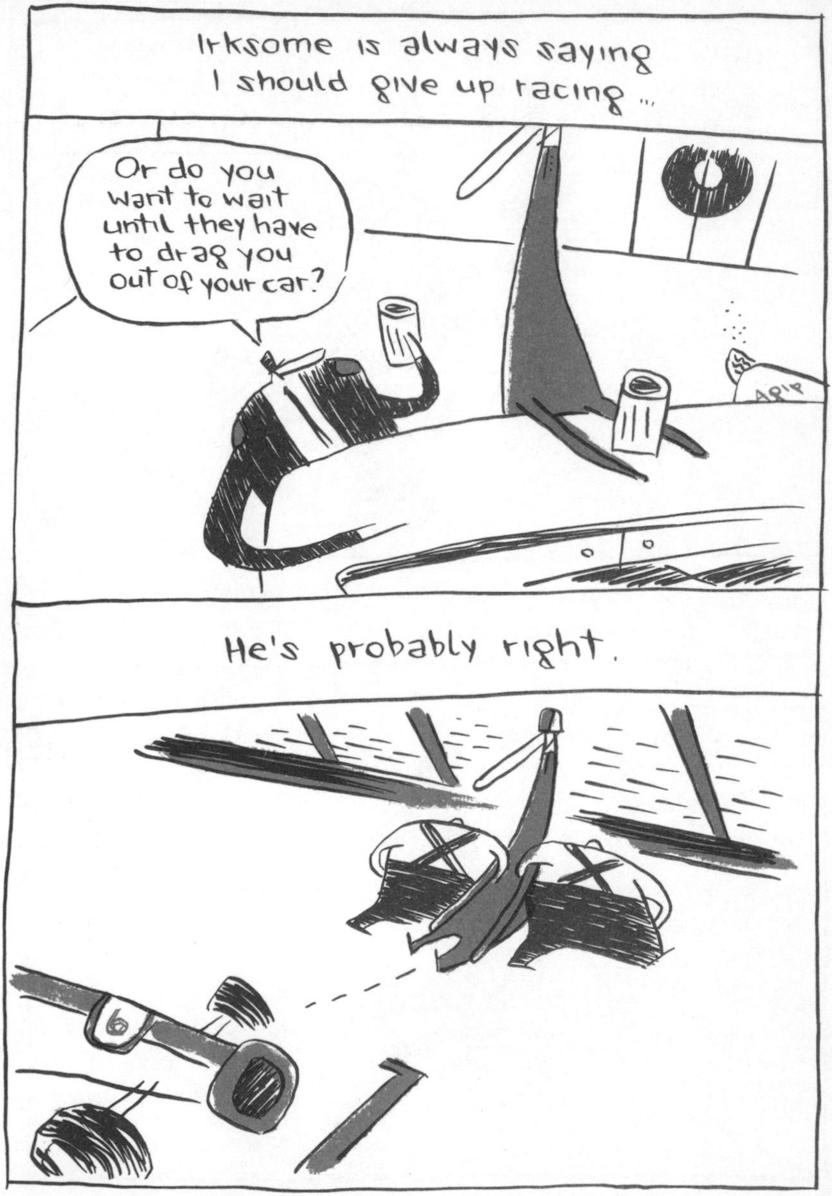

Irksome is always saying I should give up racing...
Or do you want to wait until they have to drag you out of your car?
He's probably right.

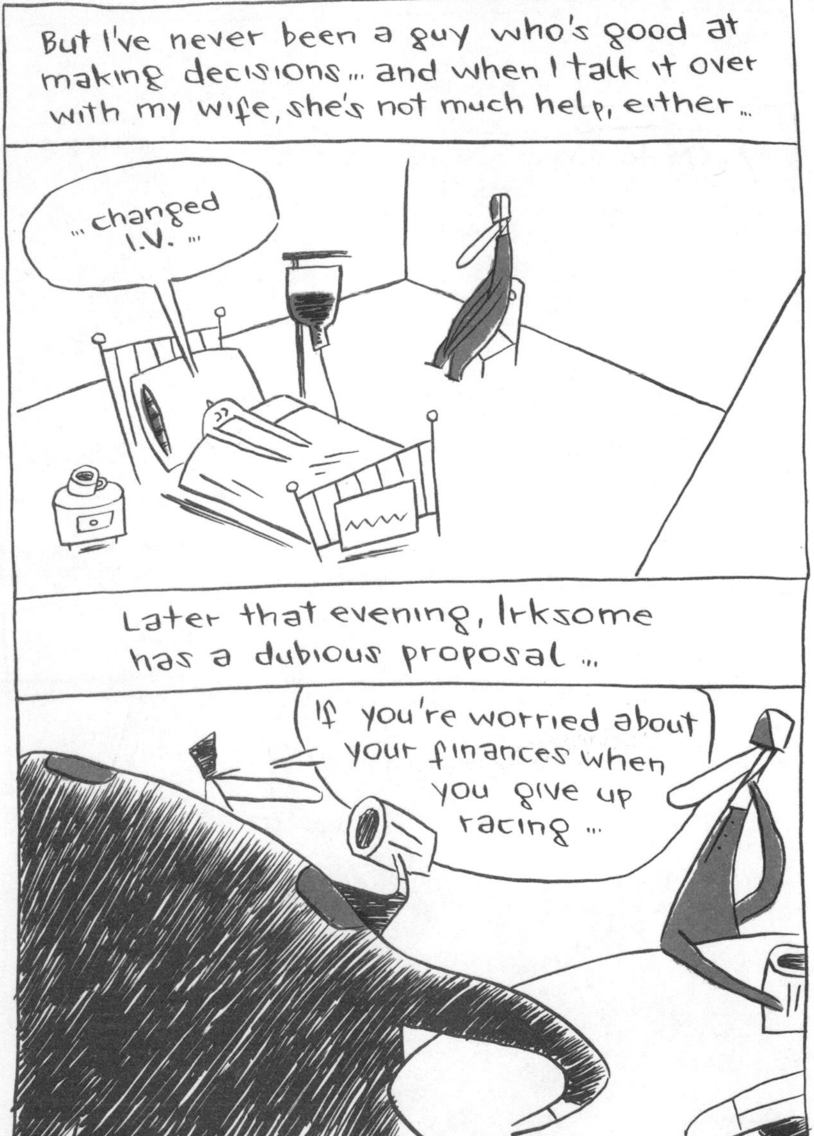
But I've never been a guy who's good at making decisions... and when I talk it over with my wife, she's not much help, either...
...changed I.V. ...
Later that evening, Irksome has a dubious proposal...
If you're worried about your finances when you give up racing...

To make a long story short, Irksome's seriously planning a bank robbery.
All I need is a getaway driver... You're first on my list...
Naturally, I'm not exactly enthusiastic about the idea...
Have you totally lost your mind? We're a pair of pretty unlikely criminals!
Believe me, it happens quicker than you think.

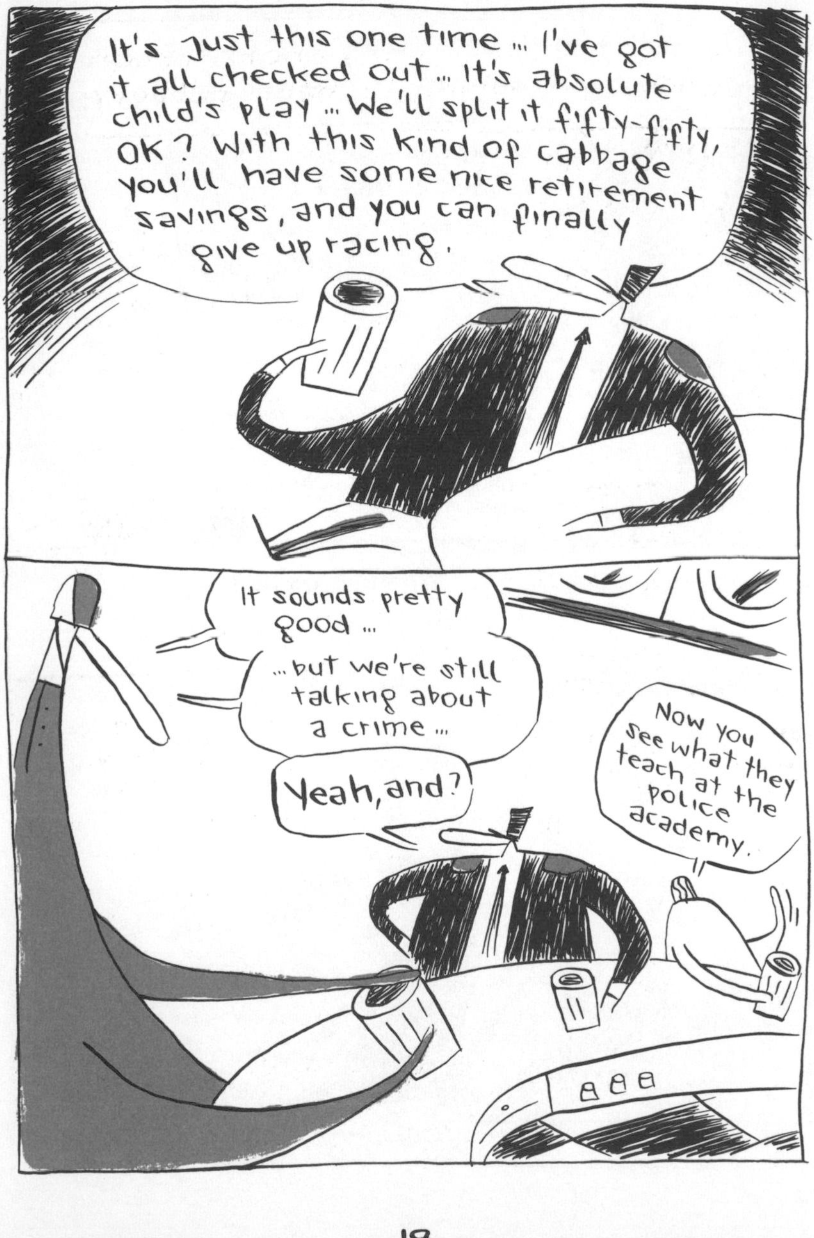
It's just this one time ... I've got it all checked out ... It's absolute child's play ... We'll split it fifty-fifty, OK? With this kind of cabbage you'll have some nice retirement savings, and you can finally give up racing.
It sounds pretty good ...
... but we're still talking about a crime ...
Yeah, and?
Now you see what they teach at the police academy.

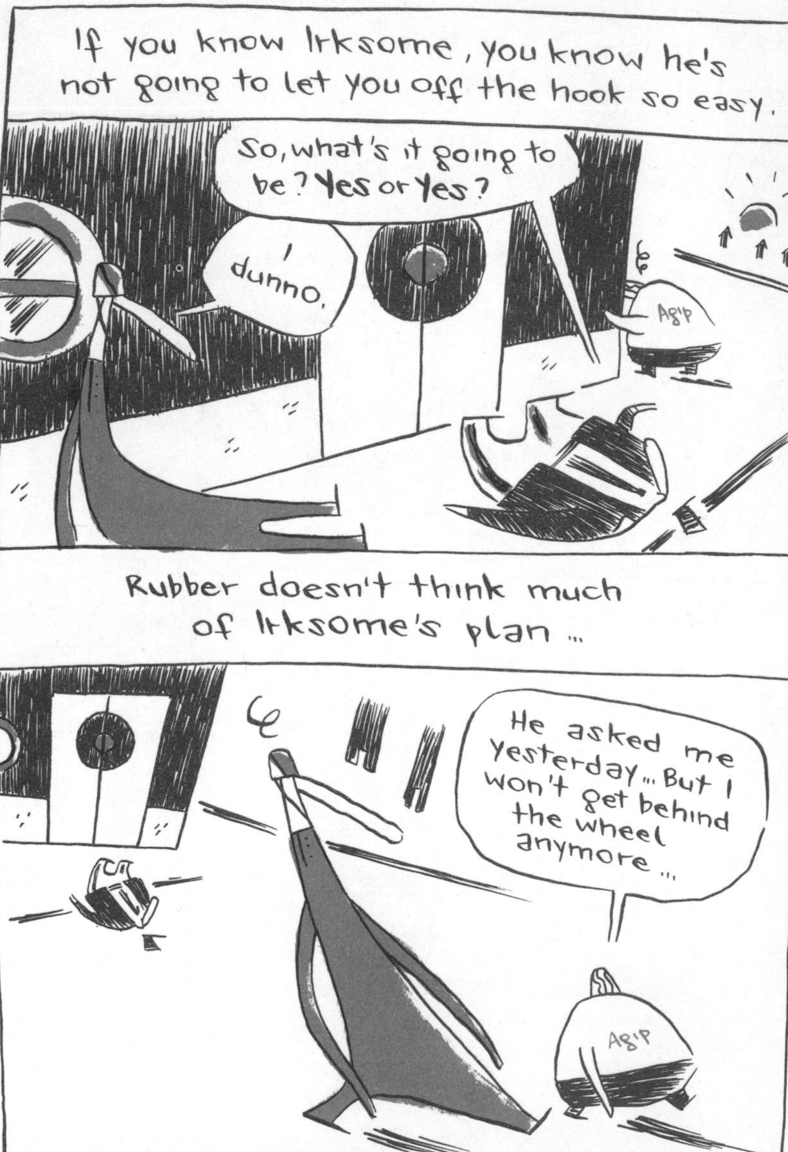
If you know Irksome, you know he's not going to let you off the hook so easy.
So, what's it going to be? Yes or Yes?
I dunno.
Rubber doesn't think much of Irksome's plan ...
He asked me yesterday... But I won't get behind the wheel anymore...

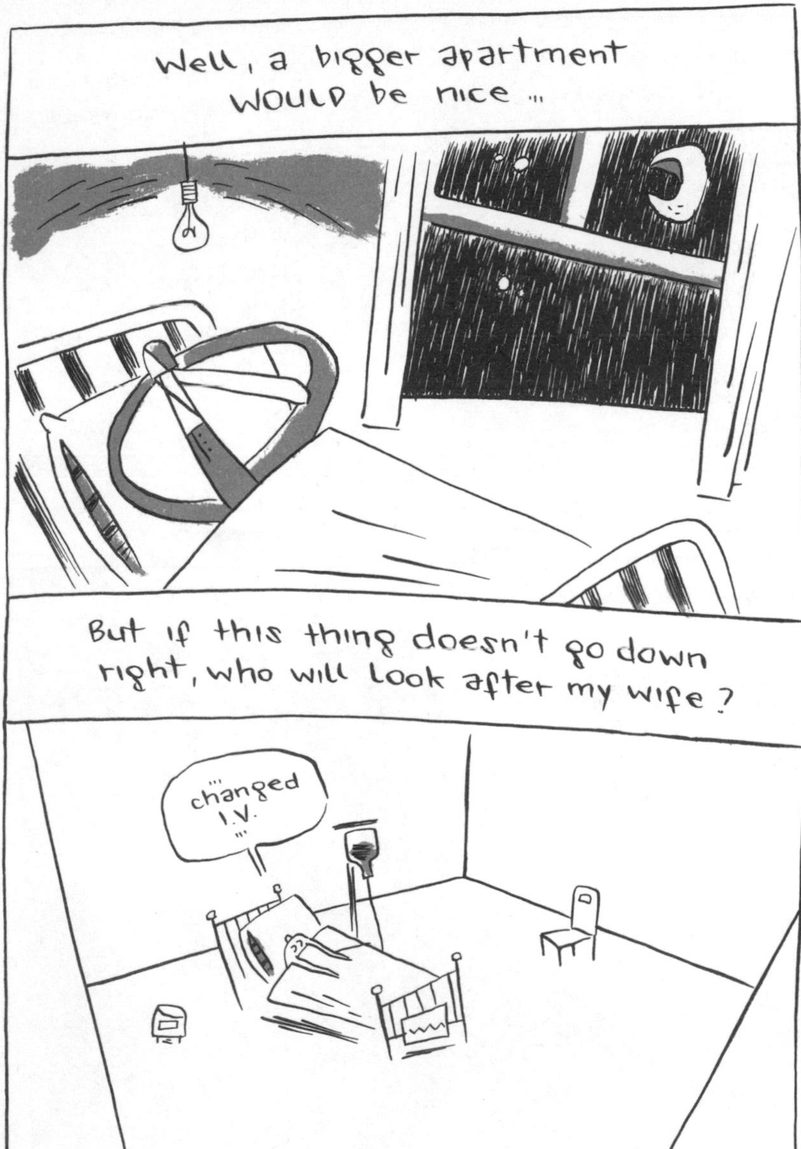
Well, a bigger apartment would be nice ...
But if this thing doesn't go down right, who will look after my wife?
... changed I.V. ...

I try to forget about the whole thing ... and go on with my life ...
Still haven't found a sponsor, you loser ?!
BAR JUA

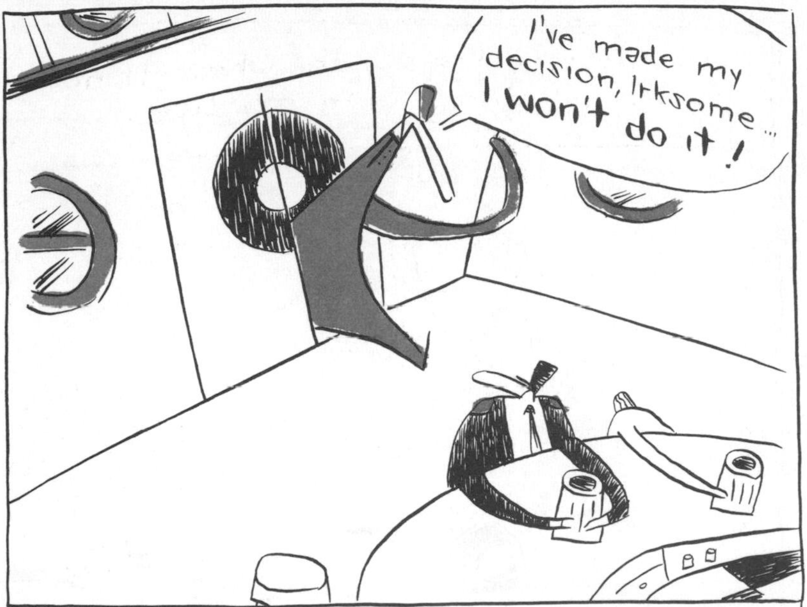
I've made my decision, Irksome... I won't do it!

Eight beers later I'm a bit mellower...

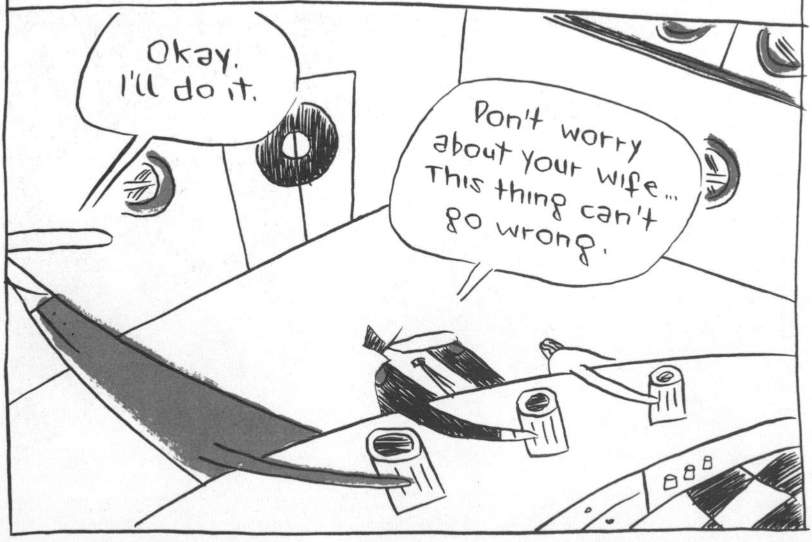
Okay. I'll do it.
Don't worry about your wife... This thing can't go wrong.

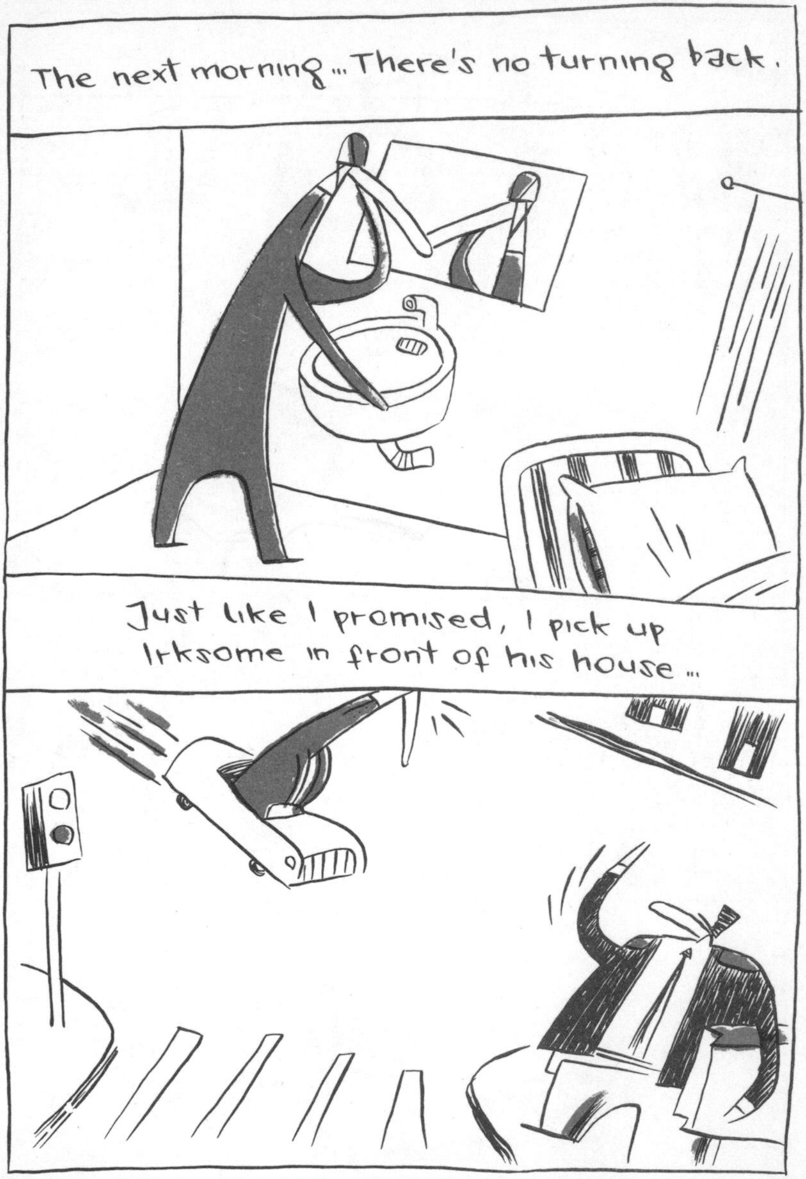
The next morning... There's no turning back.
Just like I promised, I pick up Irksome in front of his house...

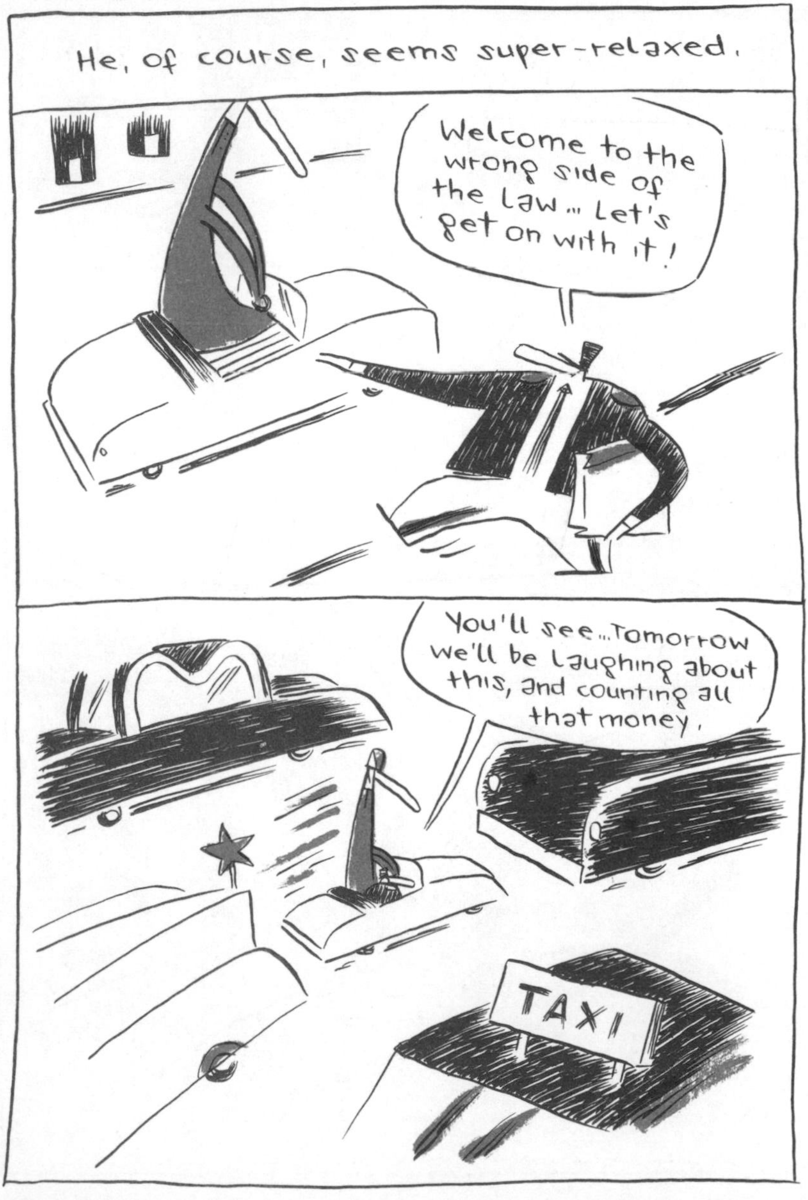
He, of course, seems super-relaxed.
Welcome to the wrong side of the law... Let's get on with it!
You'll see...Tomorrow we'll be laughing about this, and counting all that money.
TAXI

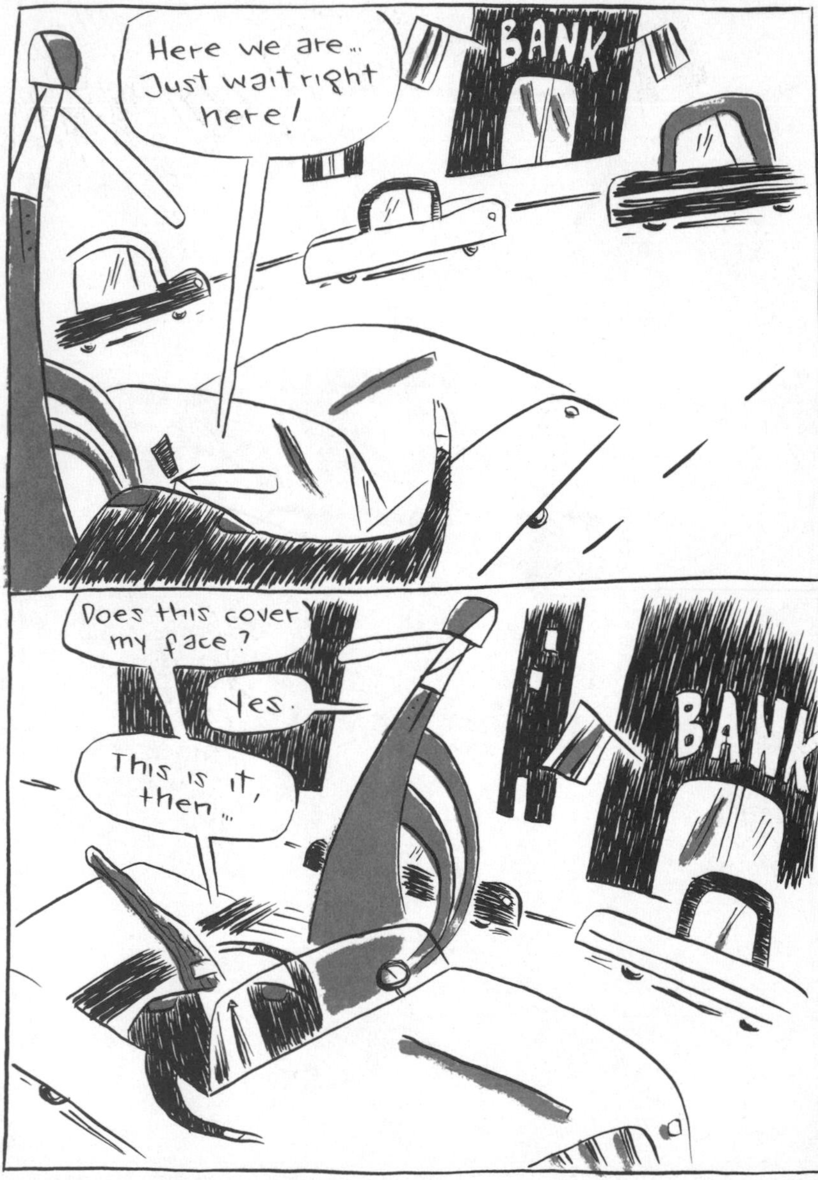
Here we are... Just wait right here!
BANK
Does this cover my face?
Yes.
This is it, then...
BANK

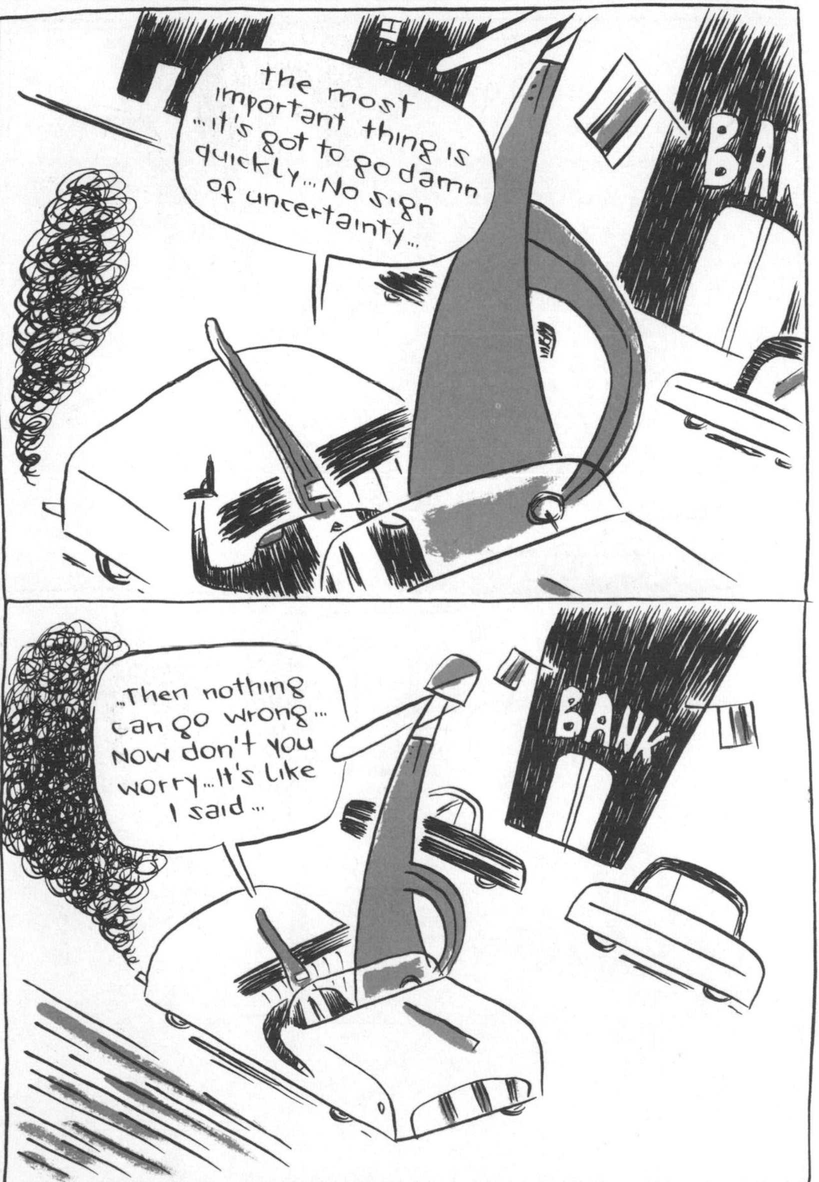
the most important thing is ...it's got to go damn quickly... No sign of uncertainty...
BA
BANK
...Then nothing can go wrong... Now don't you worry... It's like I said...

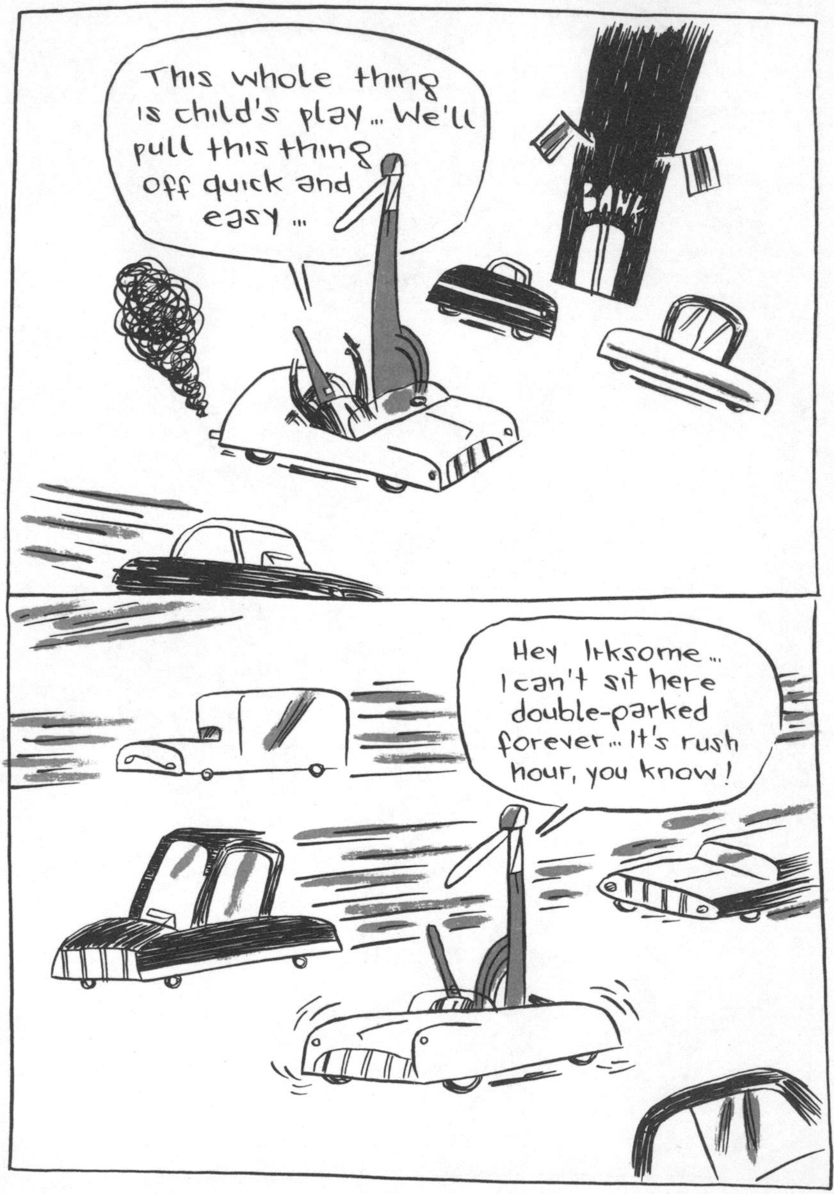
This whole thing is child's play... We'll pull this thing off quick and easy...
BANK
Hey Irksome... I can't sit here double-parked forever... It's rush hour, you know!

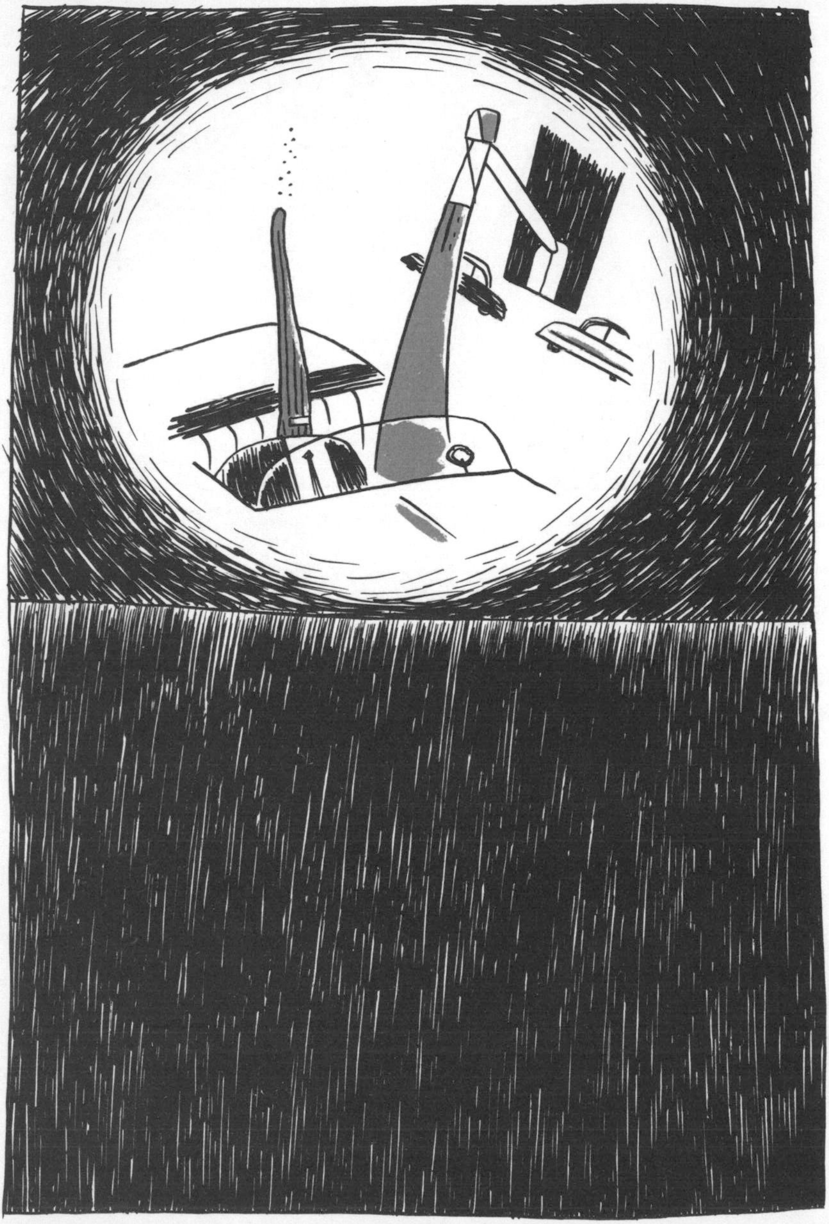

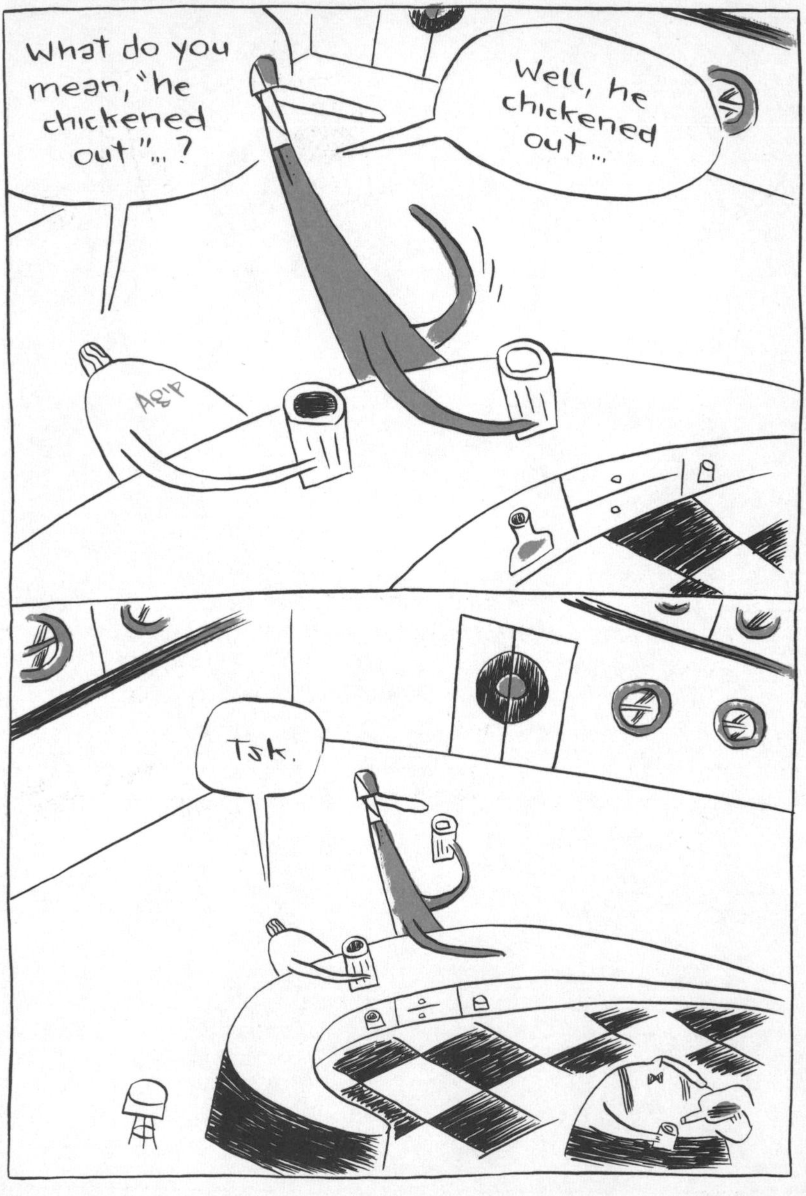
What do you mean, "he chickened out"... ?
Well, he chickened out...
Agip
Tsk.

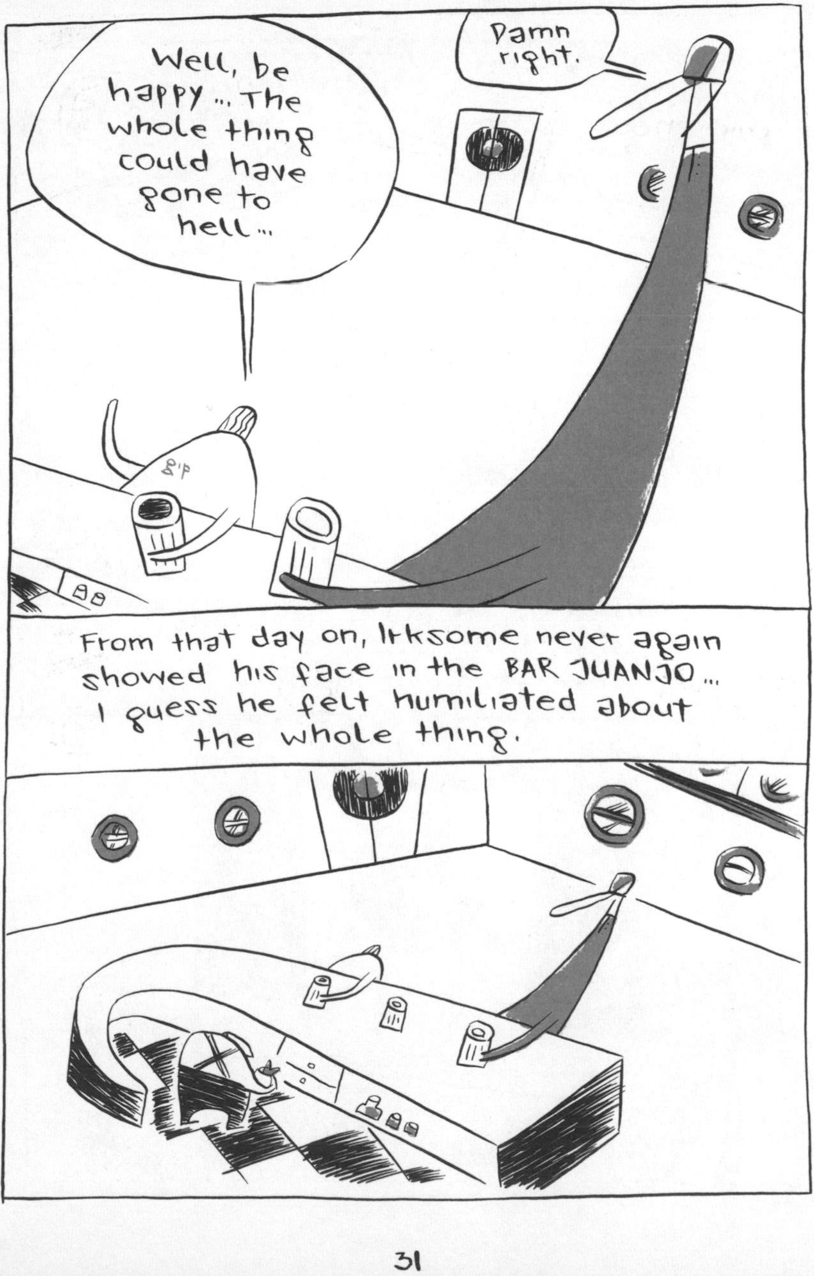
Well, be happy... The whole thing could have gone to hell...
Damn right.
From that day on, Irksome never again showed his face in the BAR JUANJO... I guess he felt humiliated about the whole thing.

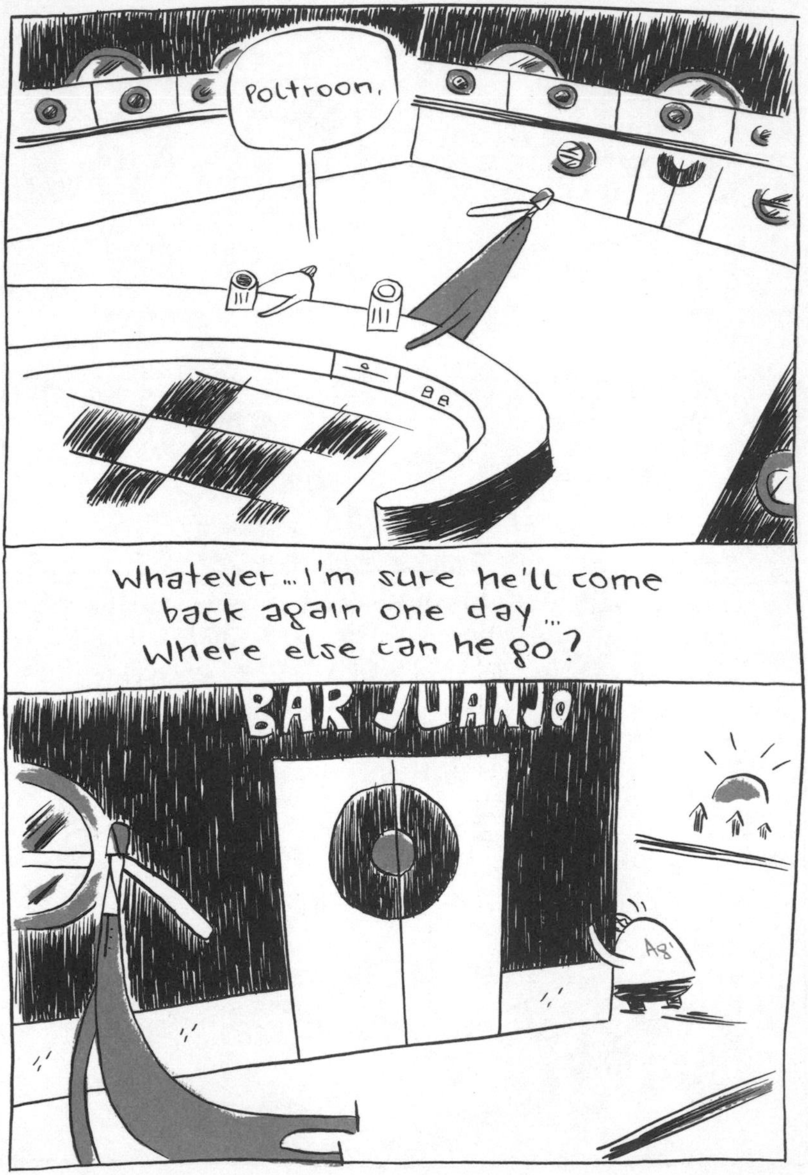
Poltroon.
Whatever... I'm sure he'll come back again one day... Where else can he go?
BAR JUANJO
Ag

2

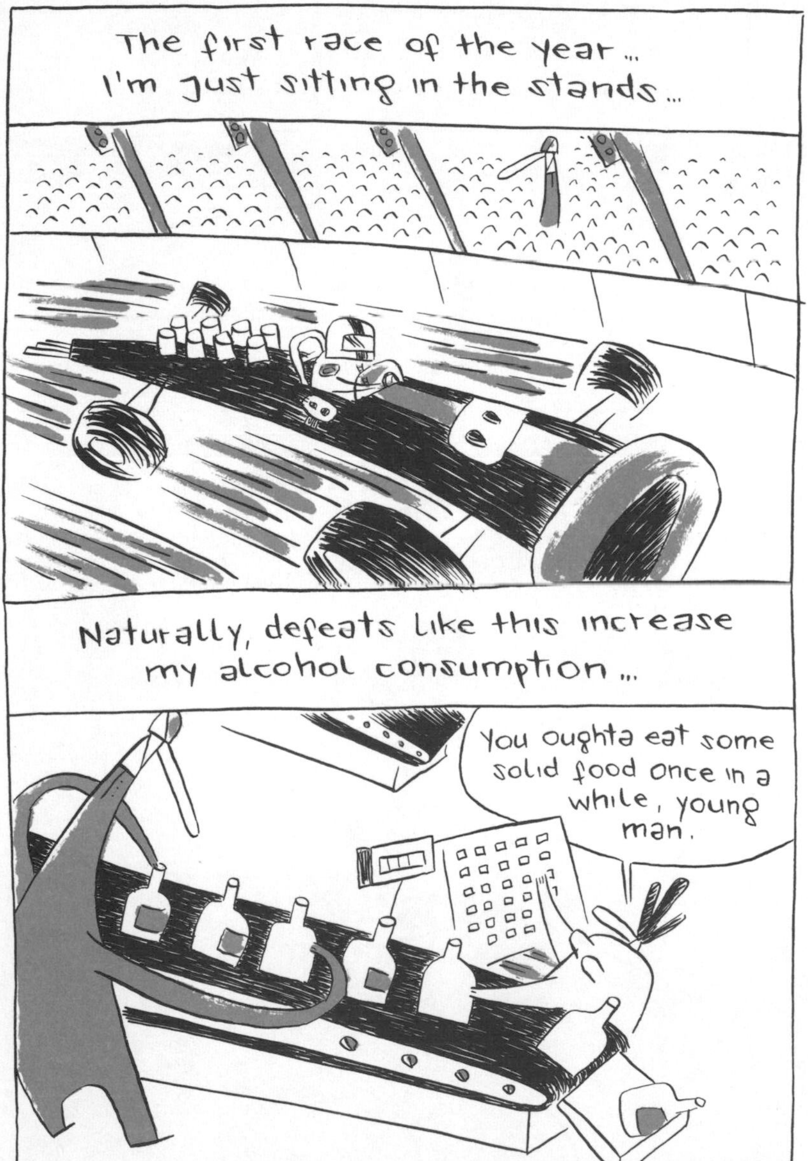
The first race of the year ...
I'm just sitting in the stands ...
Naturally, defeats like this increase my alcohol consumption ...
You oughta eat some solid food once in a while, young man.

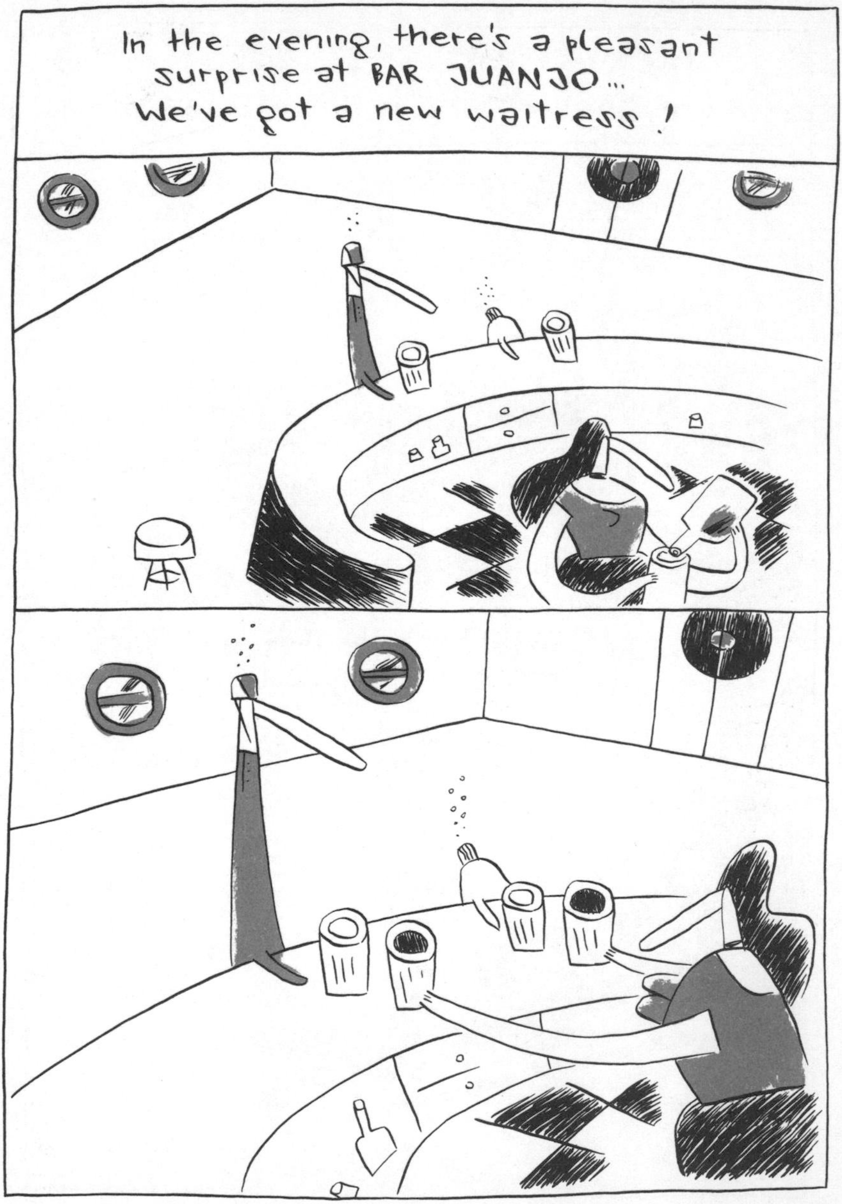
In the evening, there's a pleasant surprise at BAR JUANJO... We've got a new waitress!

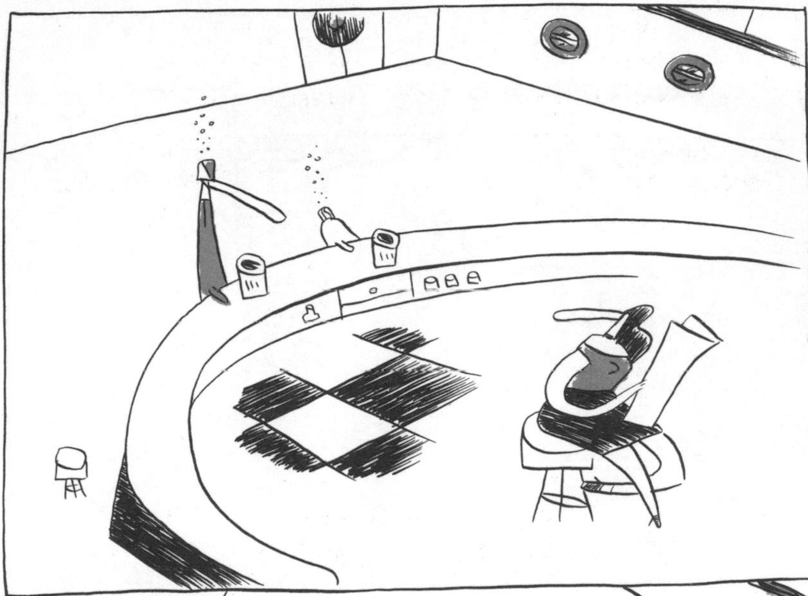

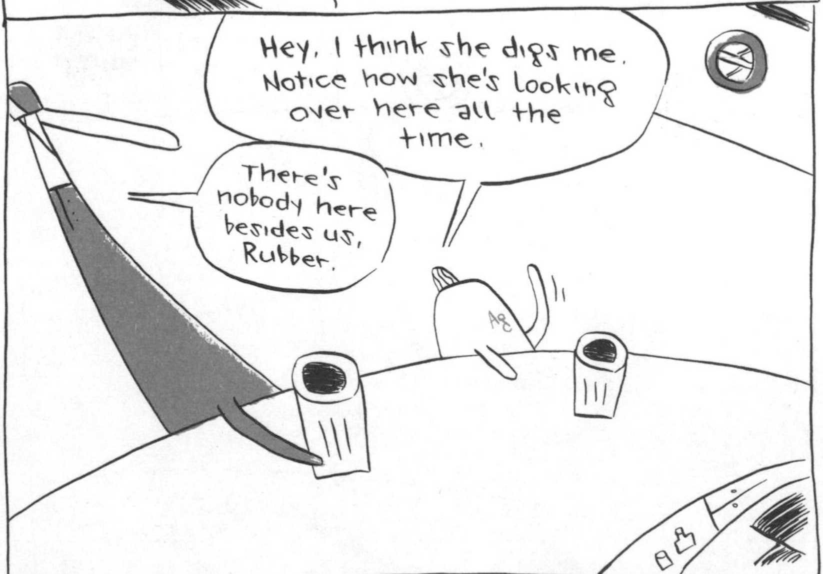
Hey, I think she digs me. Notice how she's looking over here all the time.
There's nobody here besides us, Rubber.

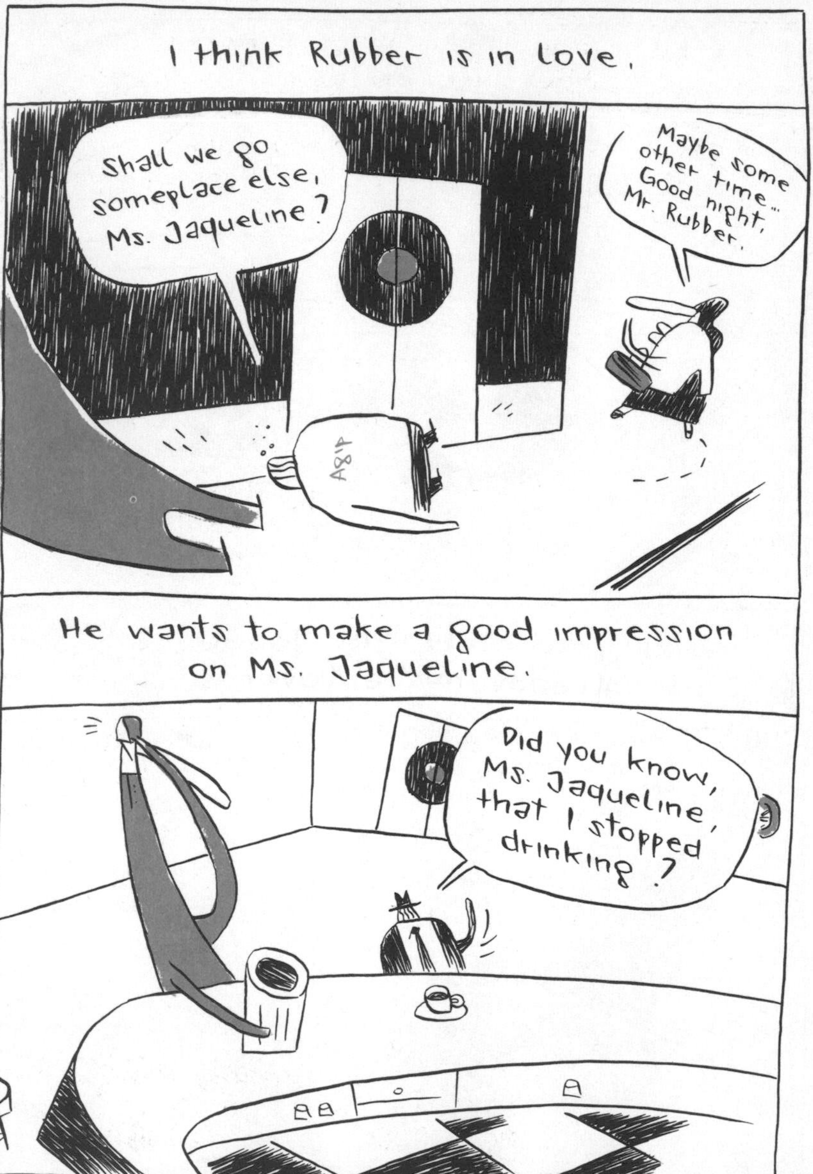
I think Rubber is in love.
Shall we go someplace else, Ms. Jaqueline?
Maybe some other time... Good night, Mr. Rubber.
He wants to make a good impression on Ms. Jaqueline.
Did you know, Ms. Jaqueline, that I stopped drinking?

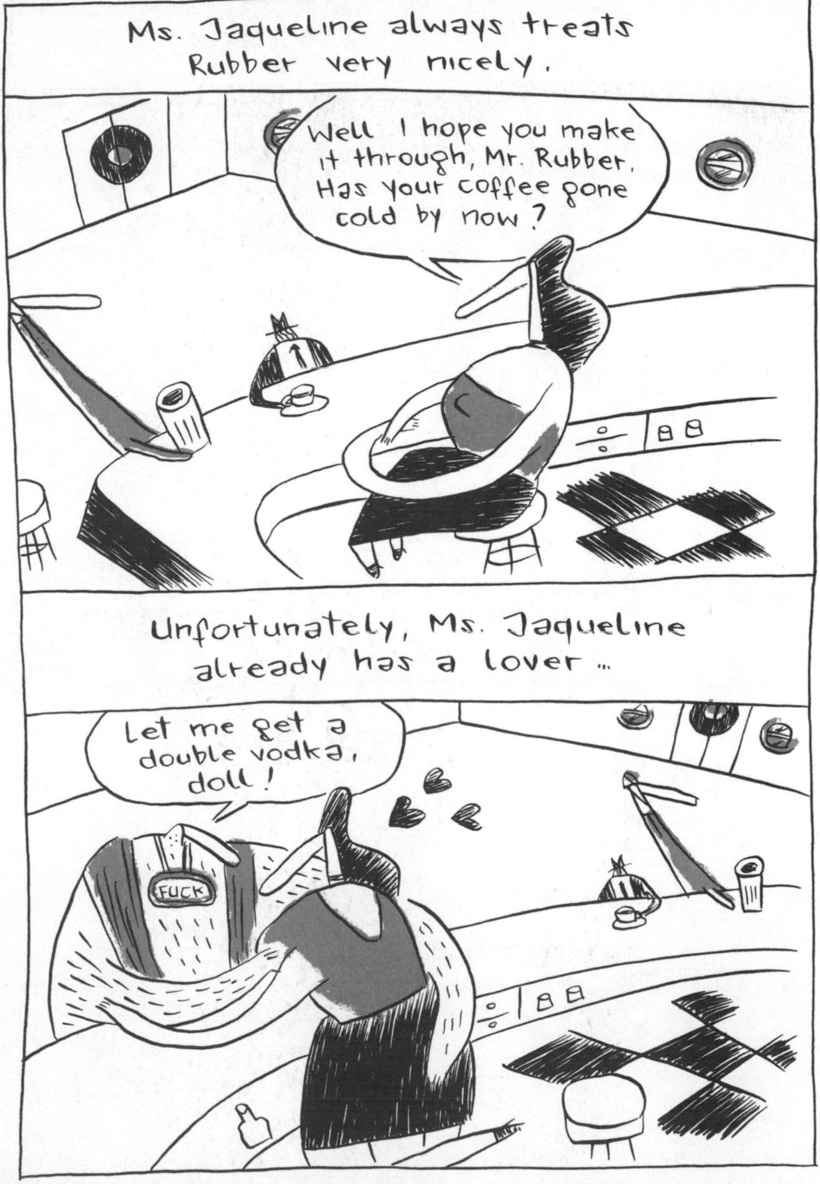
Ms. Jaqueline always treats Rubber very nicely.
Well I hope you make it through, Mr. Rubber. Has your coffee gone cold by now?
Unfortunately, Ms. Jaqueline already has a lover...
Let me get a double vodka, doll!
FUCK

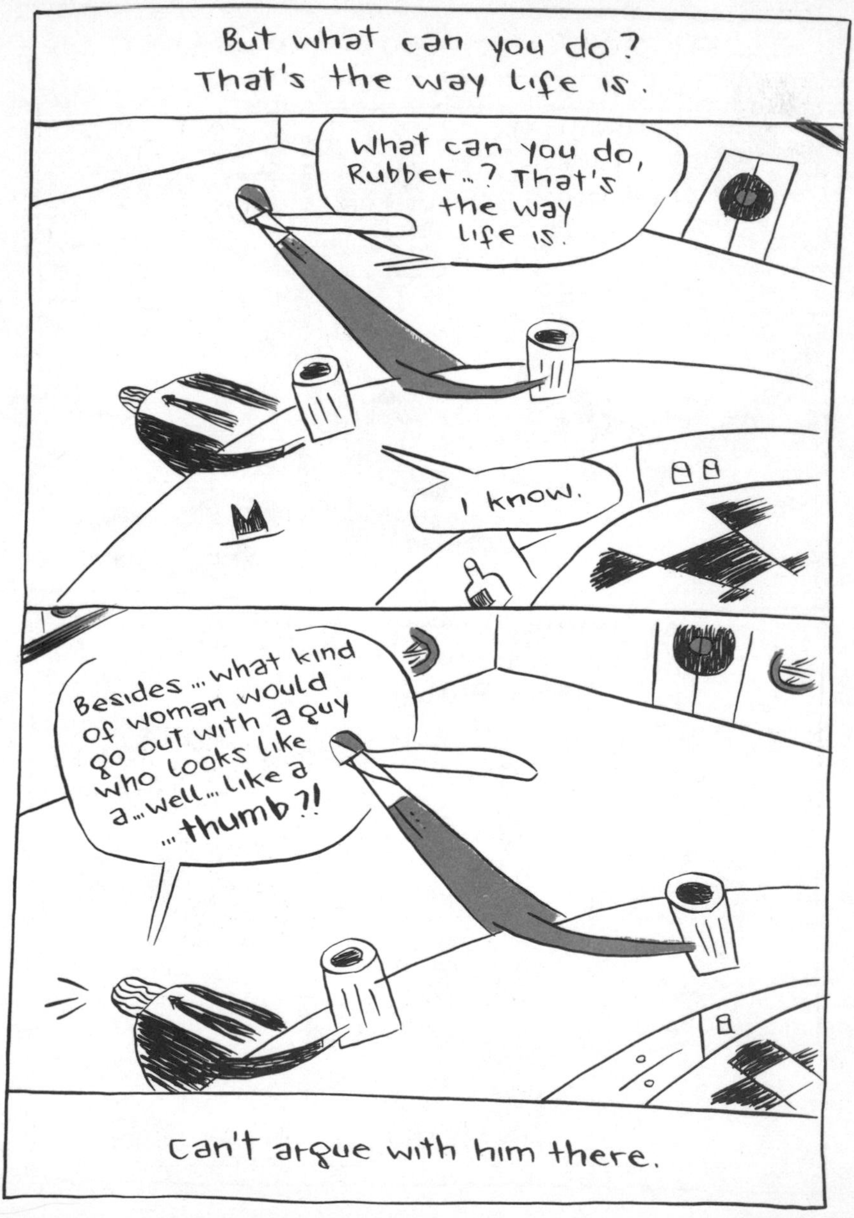
But what can you do? That's the way life is.
What can you do, Rubber...? That's the way life is.
I know.
Besides... what kind of woman would go out with a guy who looks like a...well... like a ...thumb?!
Can't argue with him there.

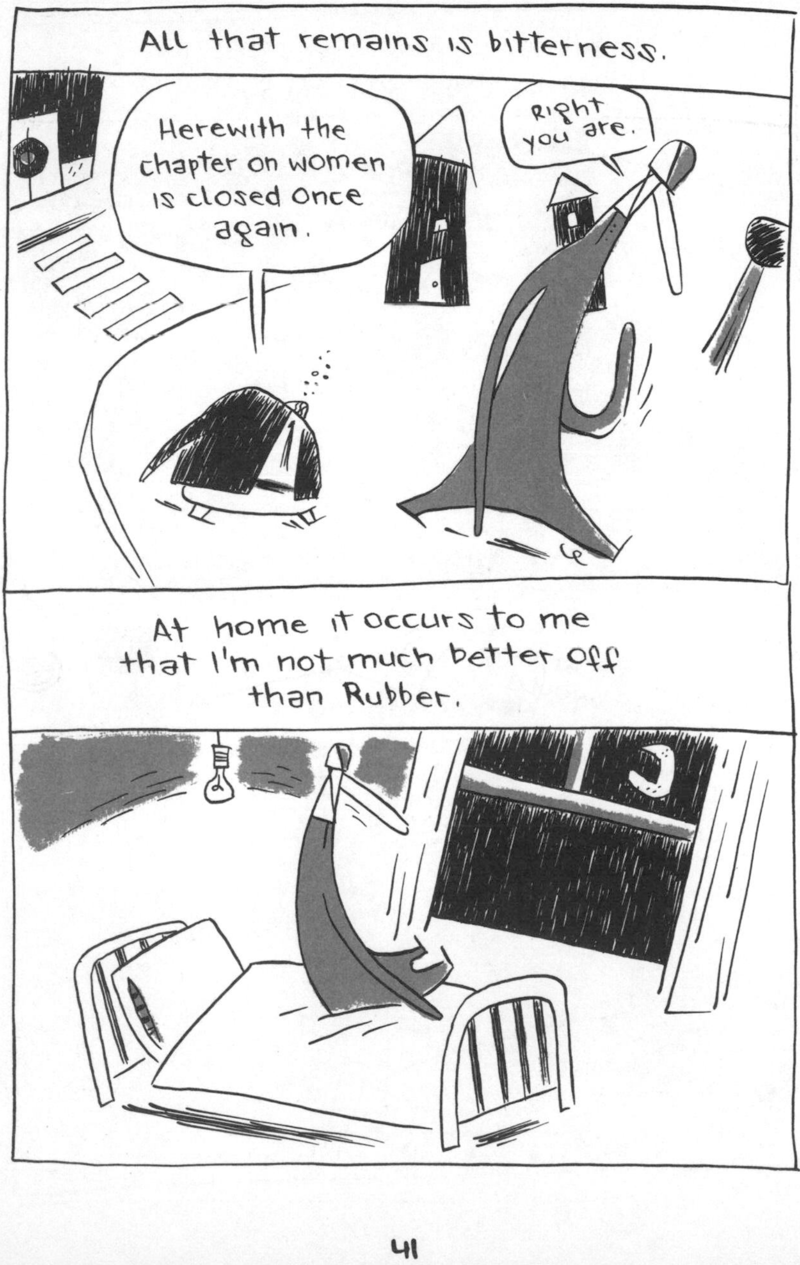
All that remains is bitterness.
Herewith the chapter on women is closed once again.
Right you are.
At home it occurs to me that I'm not much better off than Rubber.

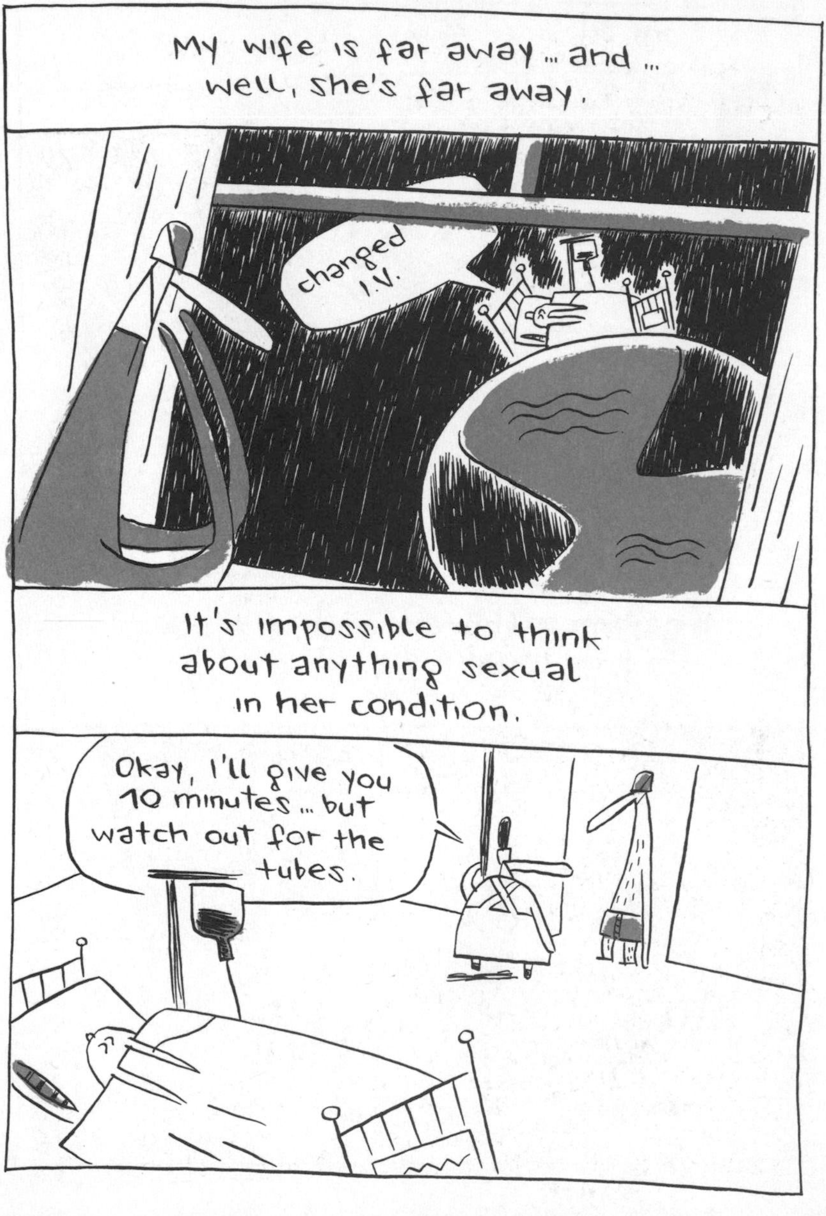
My wife is far away ... and ... well, she's far away.
changed I.V.
It's impossible to think about anything sexual in her condition.
Okay, I'll give you 10 minutes ... but watch out for the tubes.

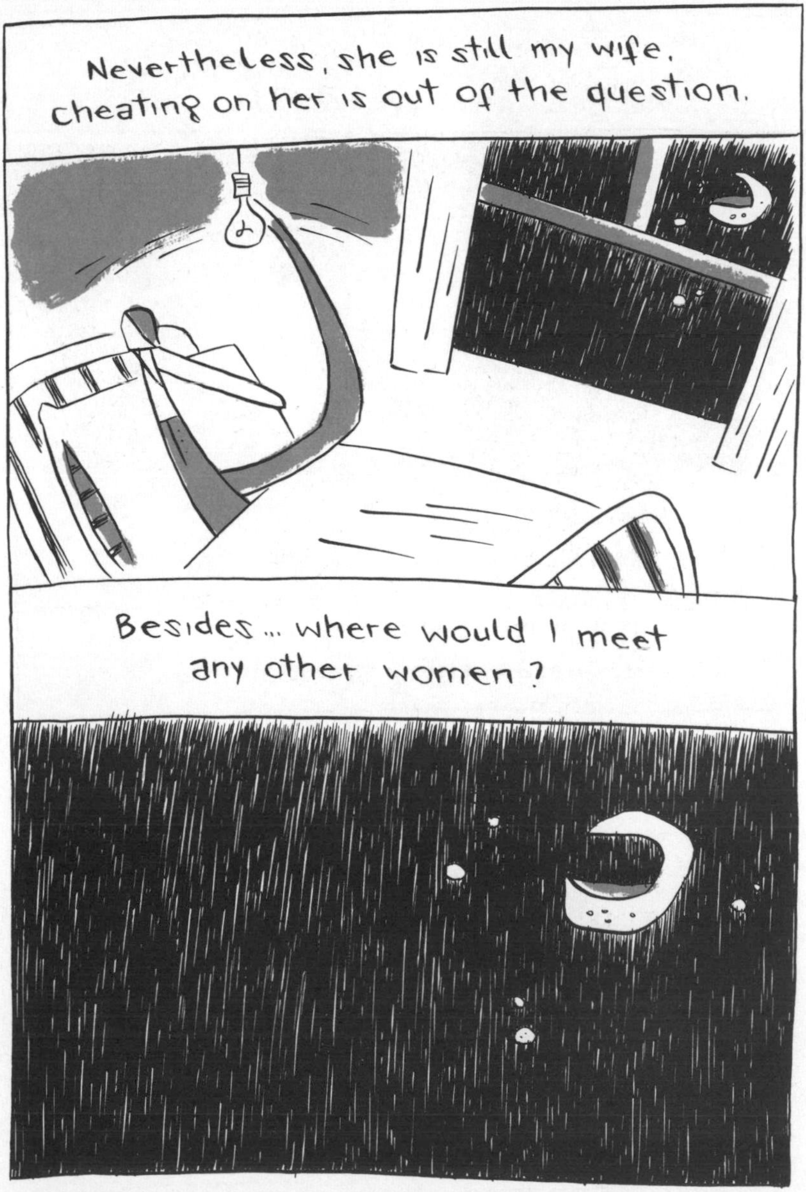
Nevertheless, she is still my wife. Cheating on her is out of the question.
Besides... where would I meet any other women?

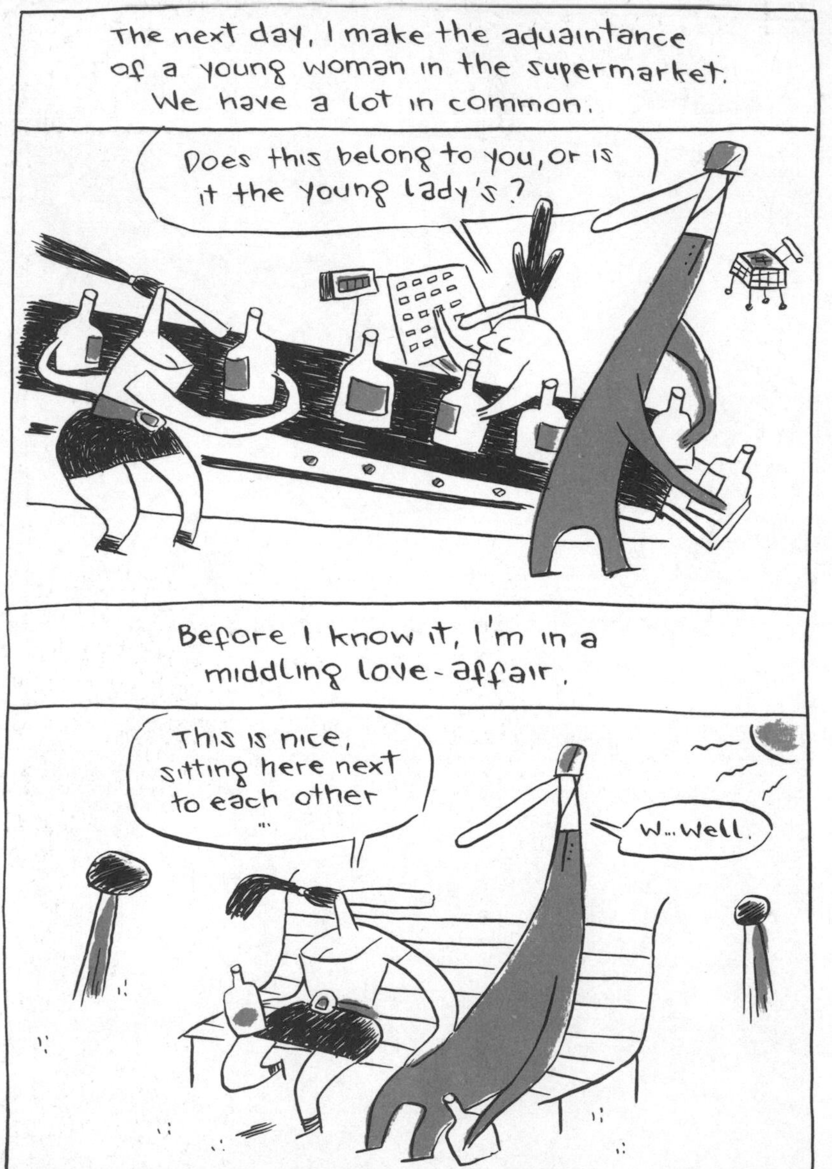
The next day, I make the aquaintance of a young woman in the supermarket. We have a lot in common.
Does this belong to you, or is it the young lady's?
Before I know it, I'm in a middling love-affair.
This is nice, sitting here next to each other ...
W... Well.

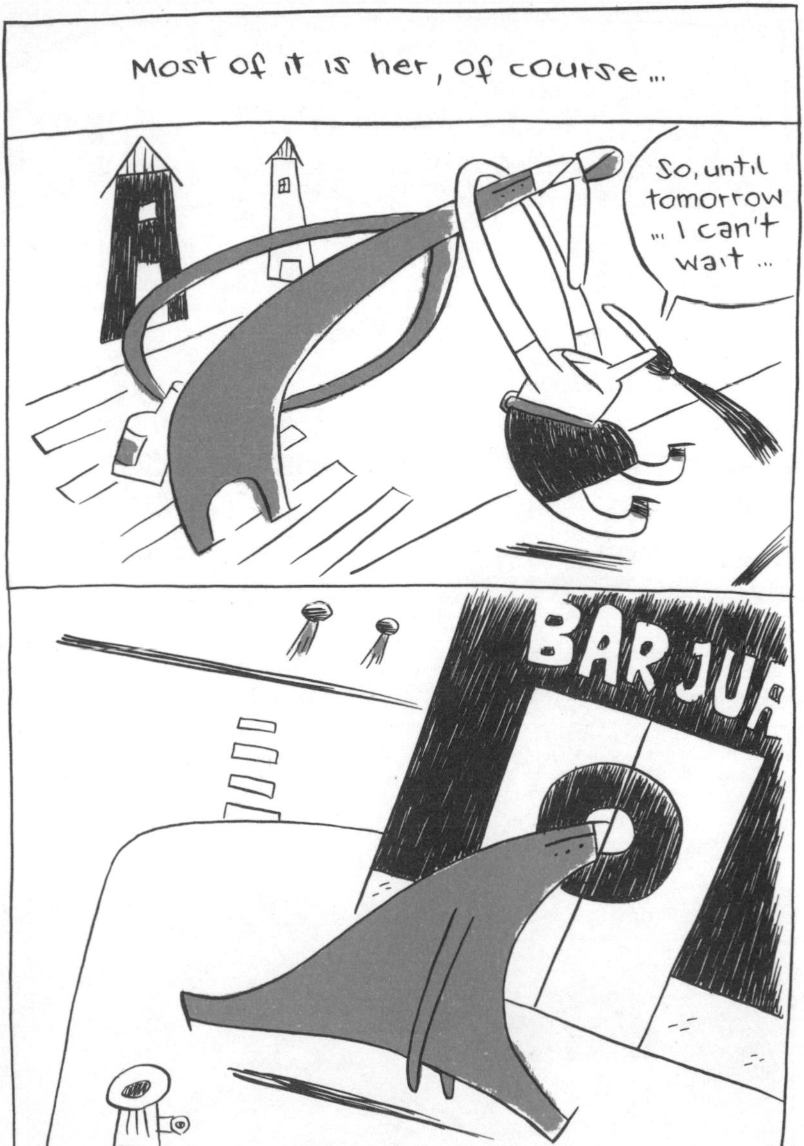
Most of it is her, of course ...
So, until tomorrow ... I can't wait ...
BAR JU

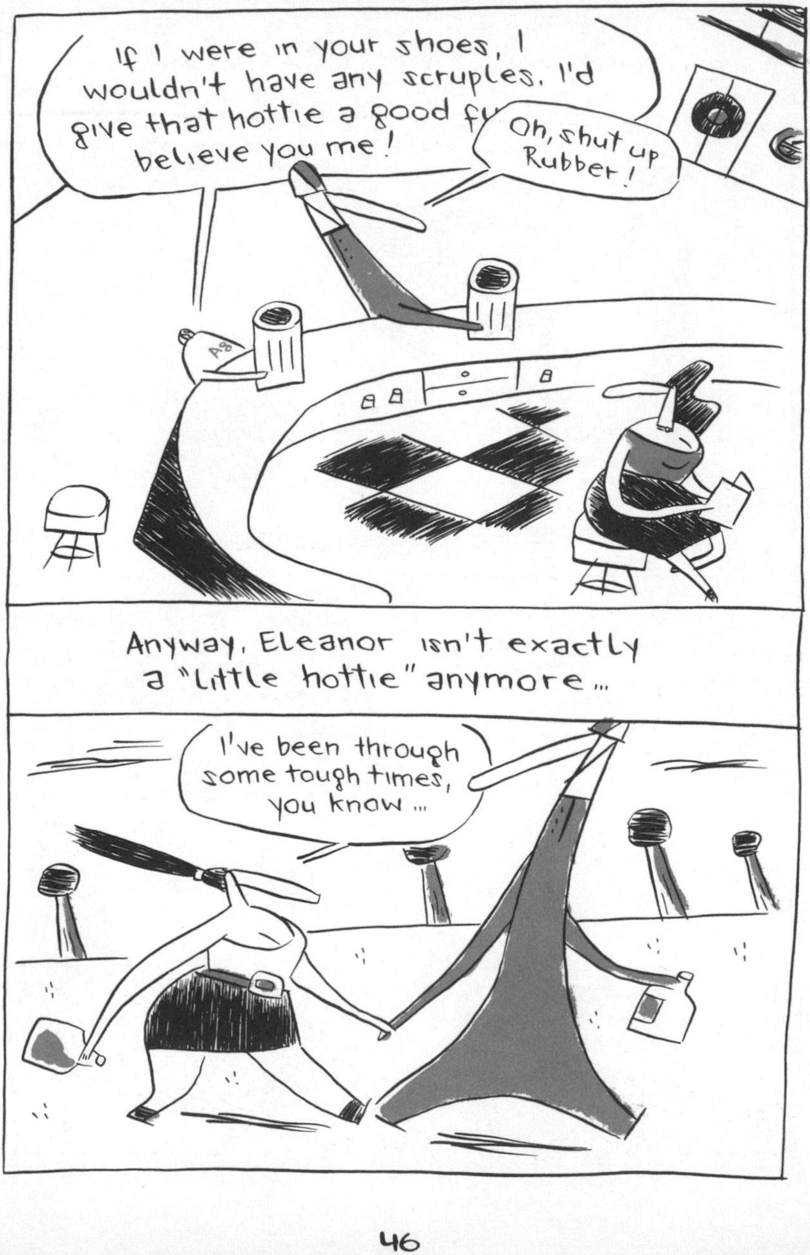
If I were in your shoes, I wouldn't have any scruples. I'd give that hottie a good fu believe you me!
Oh, shut up Rubber!
Anyway, Eleanor isn't exactly a "Little hottie" anymore...
I've been through some tough times, you know...

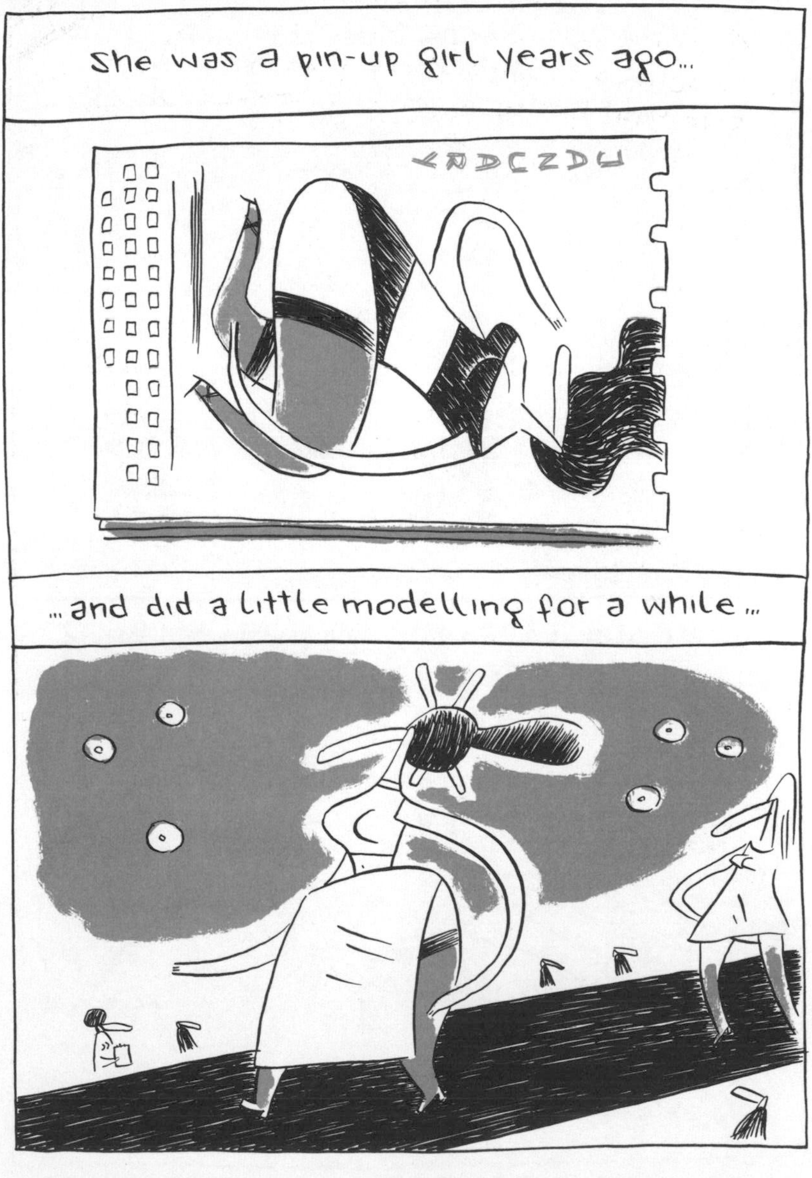
She was a pin-up girl years ago...
...and did a little modelling for a while...

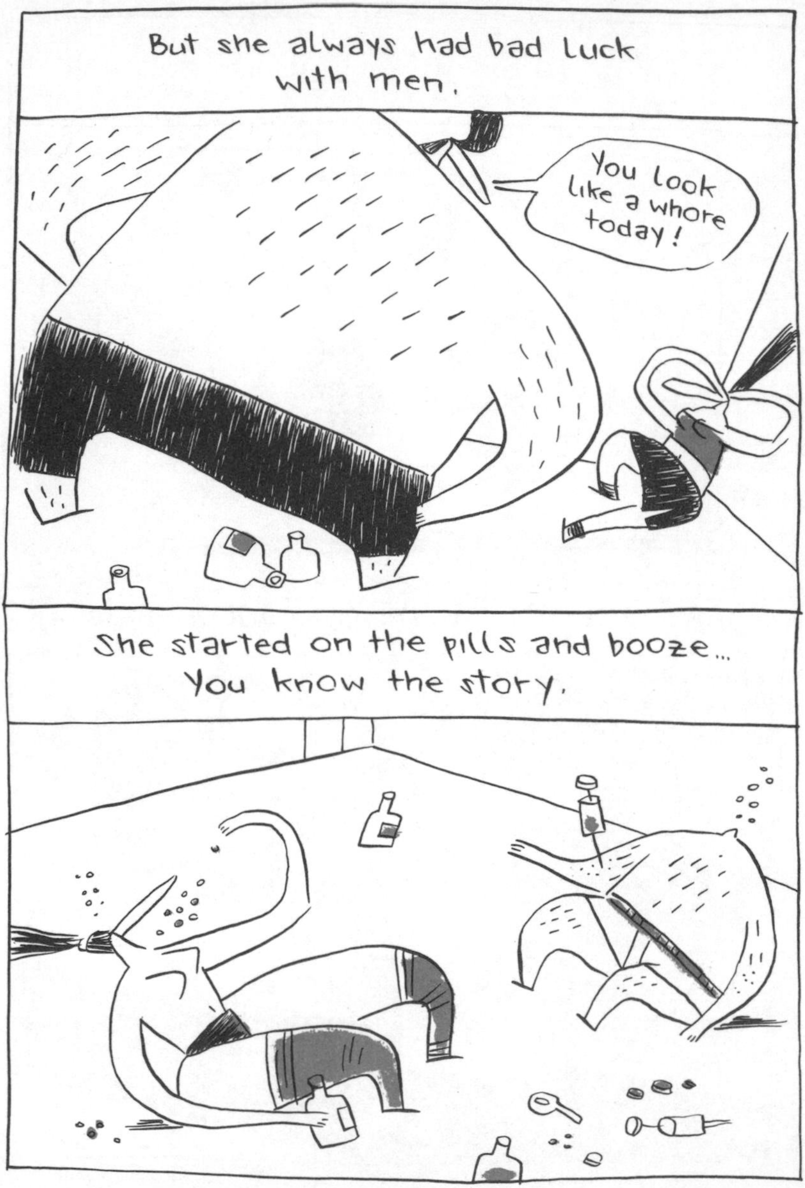
But she always had bad luck with men.
You look like a whore today!
She started on the pills and booze... You know the story.

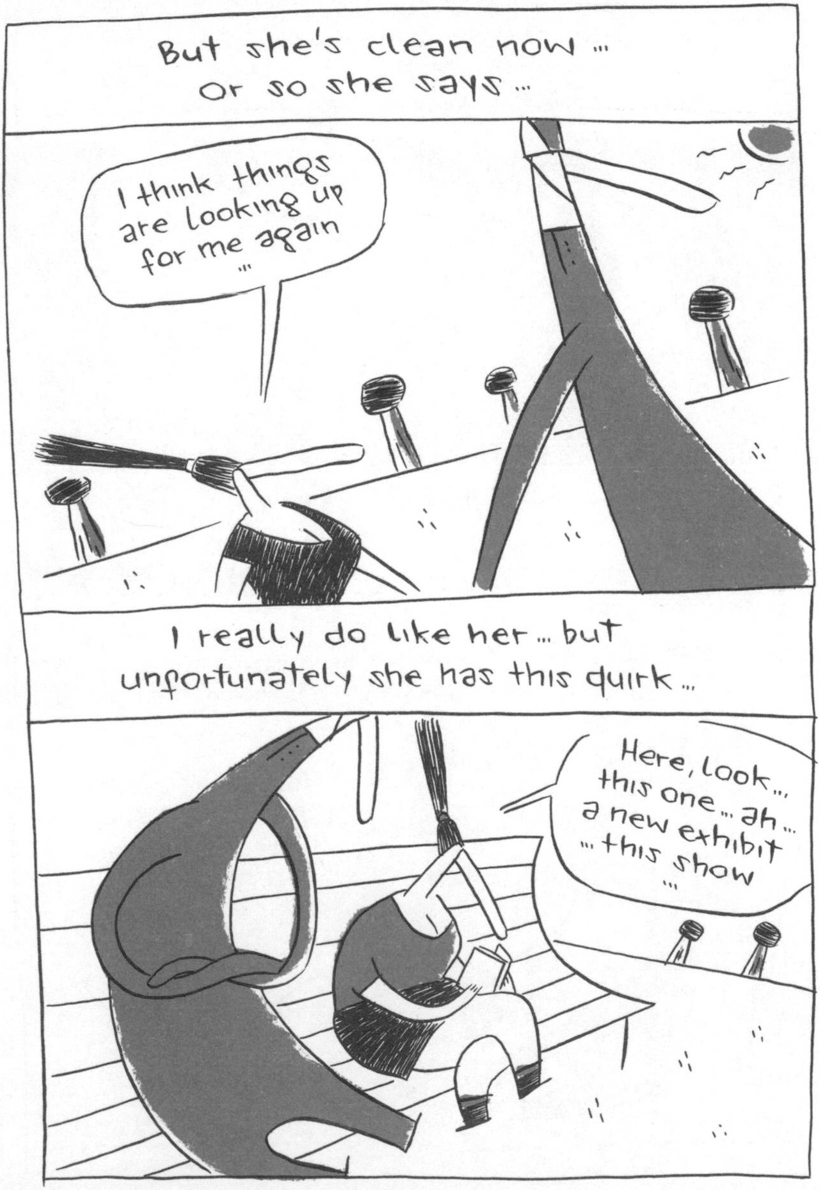
But she's clean now ... Or so she says ...
I think things are looking up for me again ...
I really do like her ... but unfortunately she has this quirk ...
Here, look ... this one ... ah ... a new exhibit ... this show ...

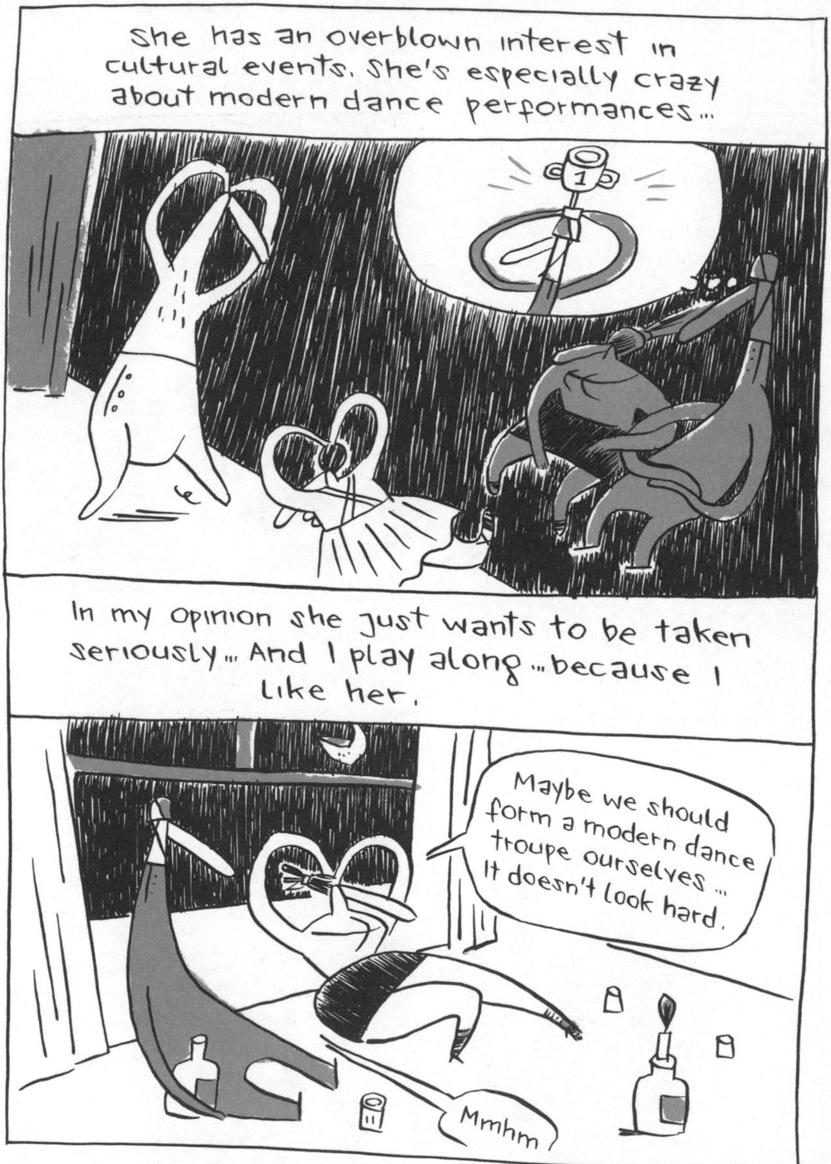

She has an overblown interest in cultural events. She's especially crazy about modern dance performances...
In my opinion she just wants to be taken seriously... And I play along... because I like her.
Maybe we should form a modern dance troupe ourselves... It doesn't look hard.
Mmhm

Of course, Rubber makes fun of me for the whole thing.
Hey, no poetry reading today?
But the poetry readings are not the worst part.
...

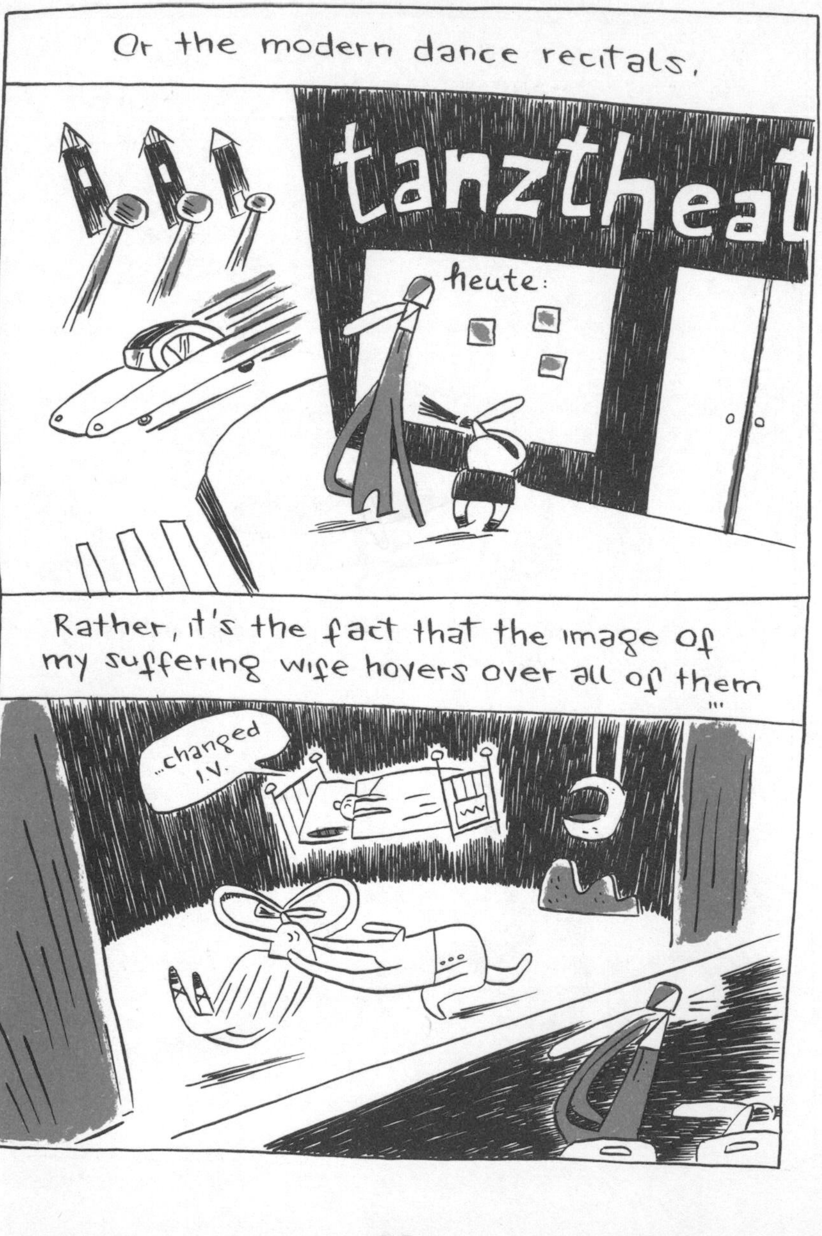
Or the modern dance recitals.
tanztheat
heute:
Rather, it's the fact that the image of my suffering wife hovers over all of them ...
...changed I.V.

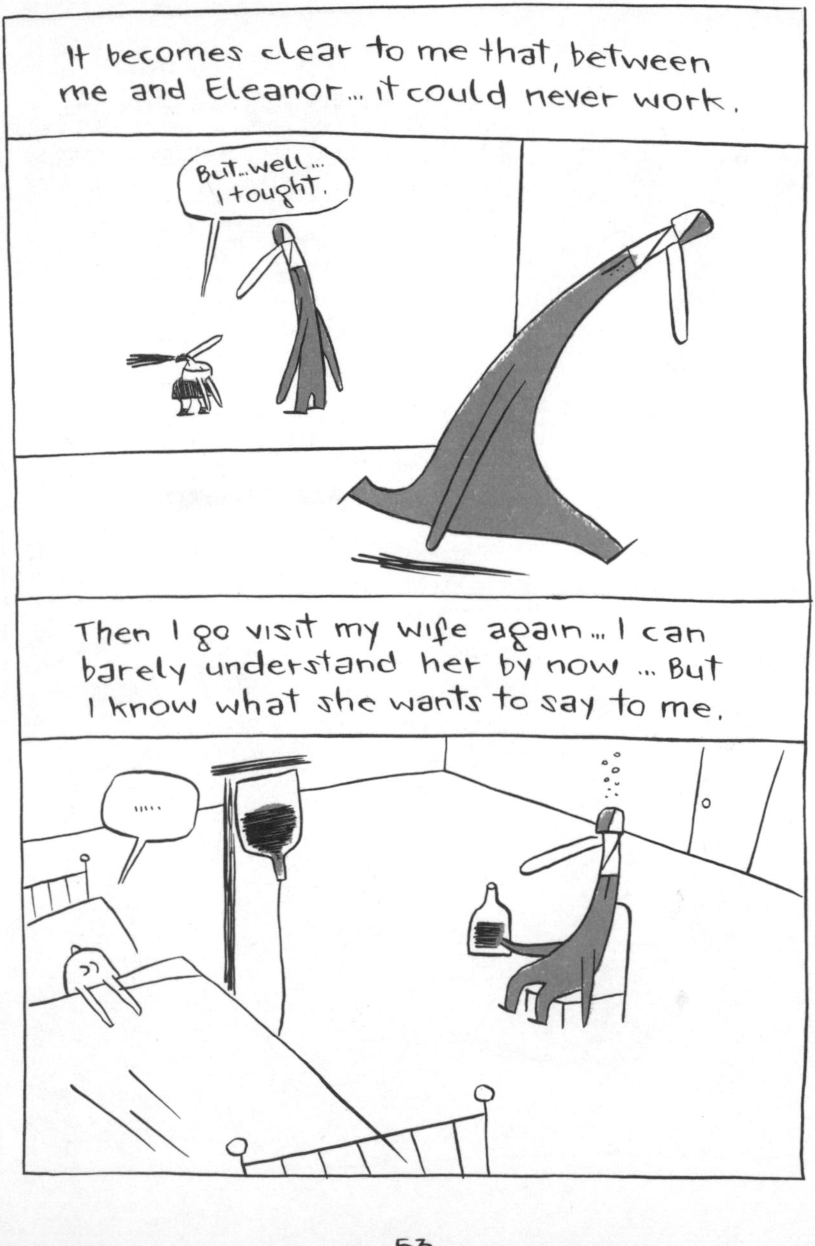
It becomes clear to me that, between me and Eleanor... it could never work.
But... well... I tought.
Then I go visit my wife again... I can barely understand her by now ... But I know what she wants to say to me.
.....

I believe that, secretly, Rubber is glad he doesn't always have to drink alone anymore.
Women can't replace alcohol, you've got to know that.
Nevertheless... You should have given that little hottie a good fu at least once!
Shut up, Rubber.
Ag'

I watch the second race of the year in a window of a TV shop ...

And of course that Delli-Ferolli wins again ...

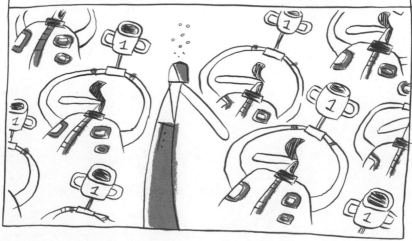

55

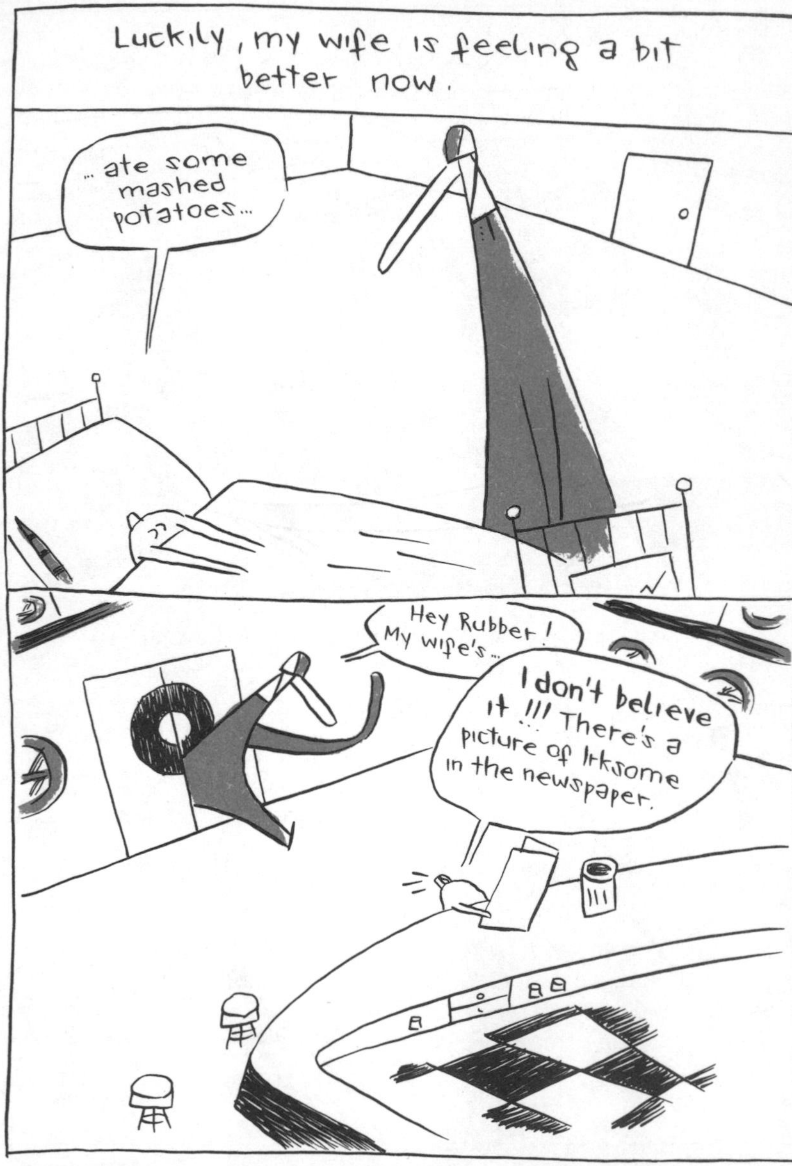
Luckily, my wife is feeling a bit better now.
... ate some mashed potatoes...
Hey Rubber! My wife's...
I don't believe it !!! There's a picture of Irksome in the newspaper.

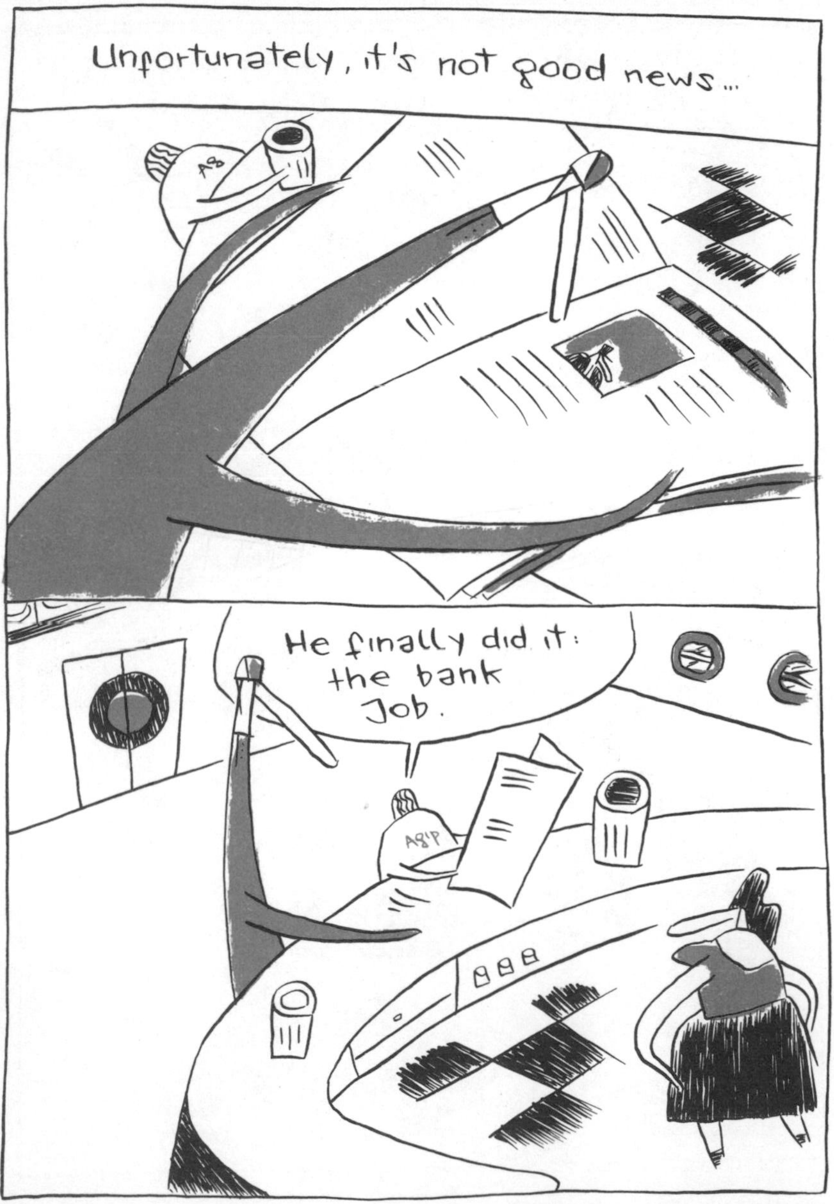
Unfortunately, it's not good news...
He finally did it: the bank Job.

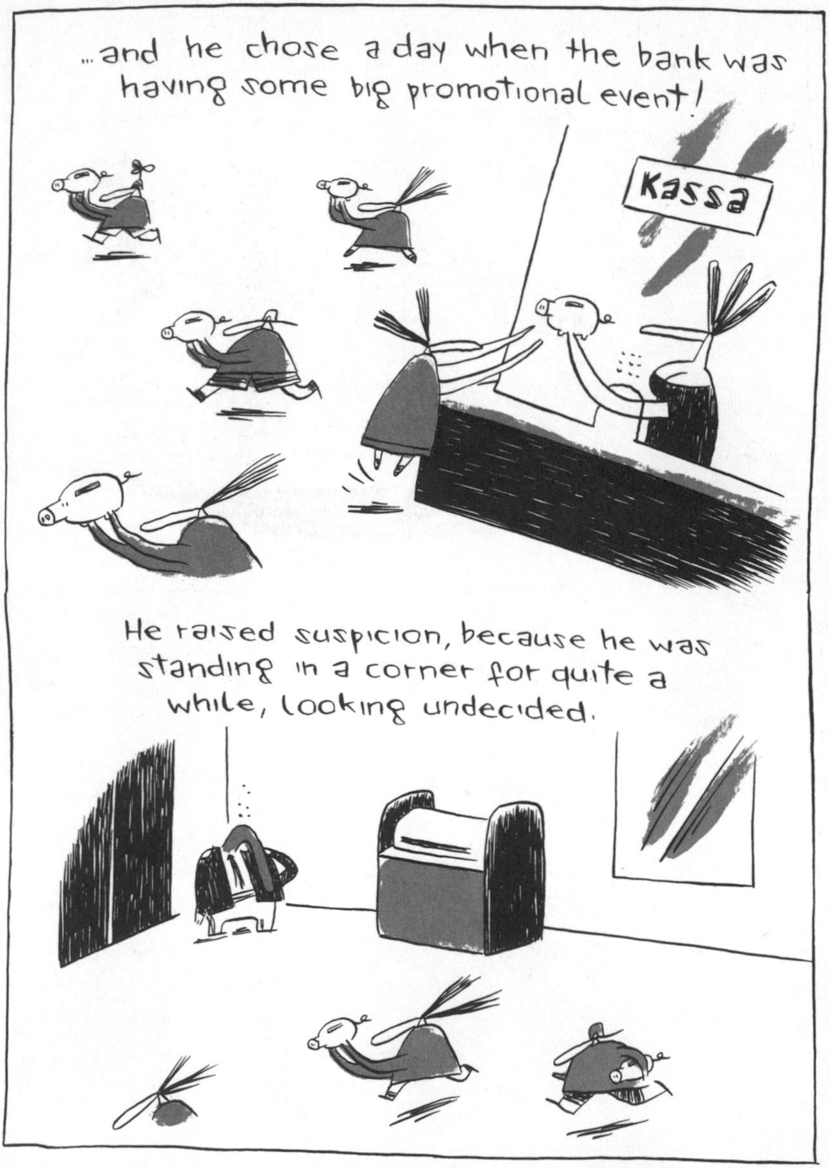
...and he chose a day when the bank was having some big promotional event!
Kassa
He raised suspicion, because he was standing in a corner for quite a while, looking undecided.

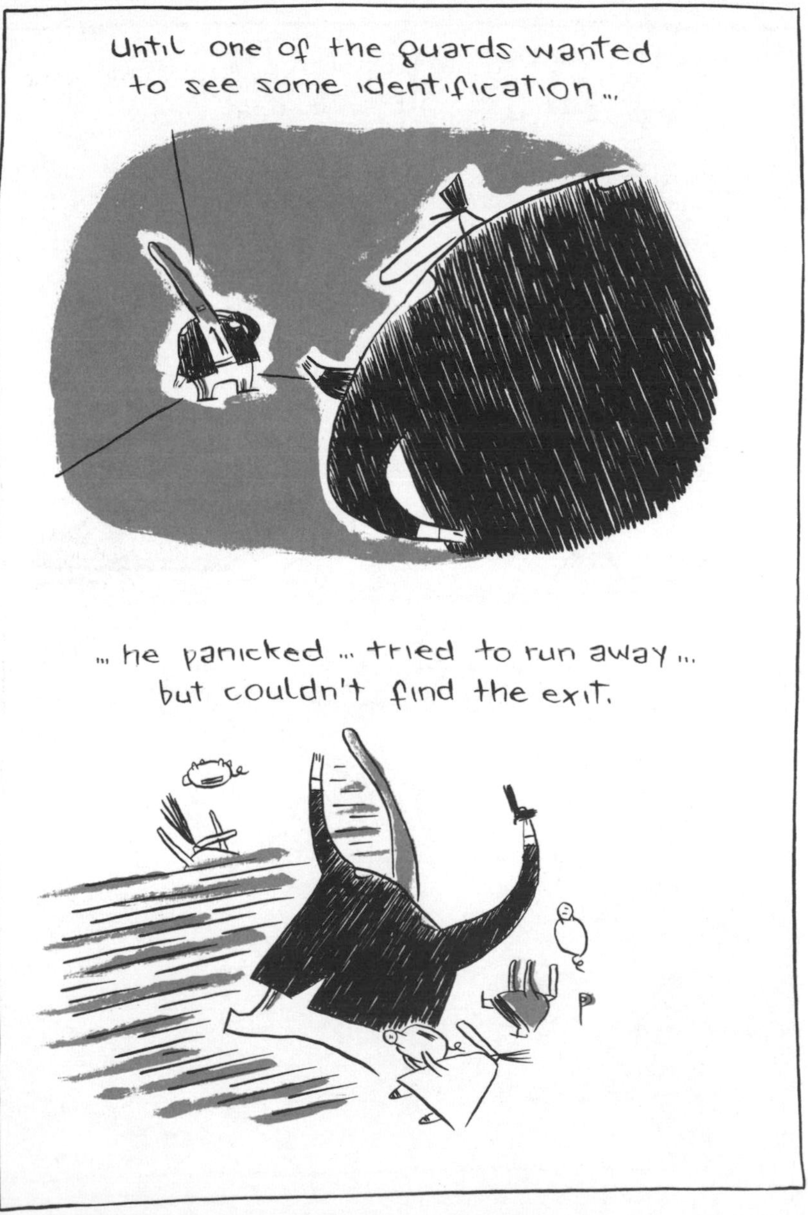
Until one of the guards wanted to see some identification...
... he panicked ... tried to run away ... but couldn't find the exit.

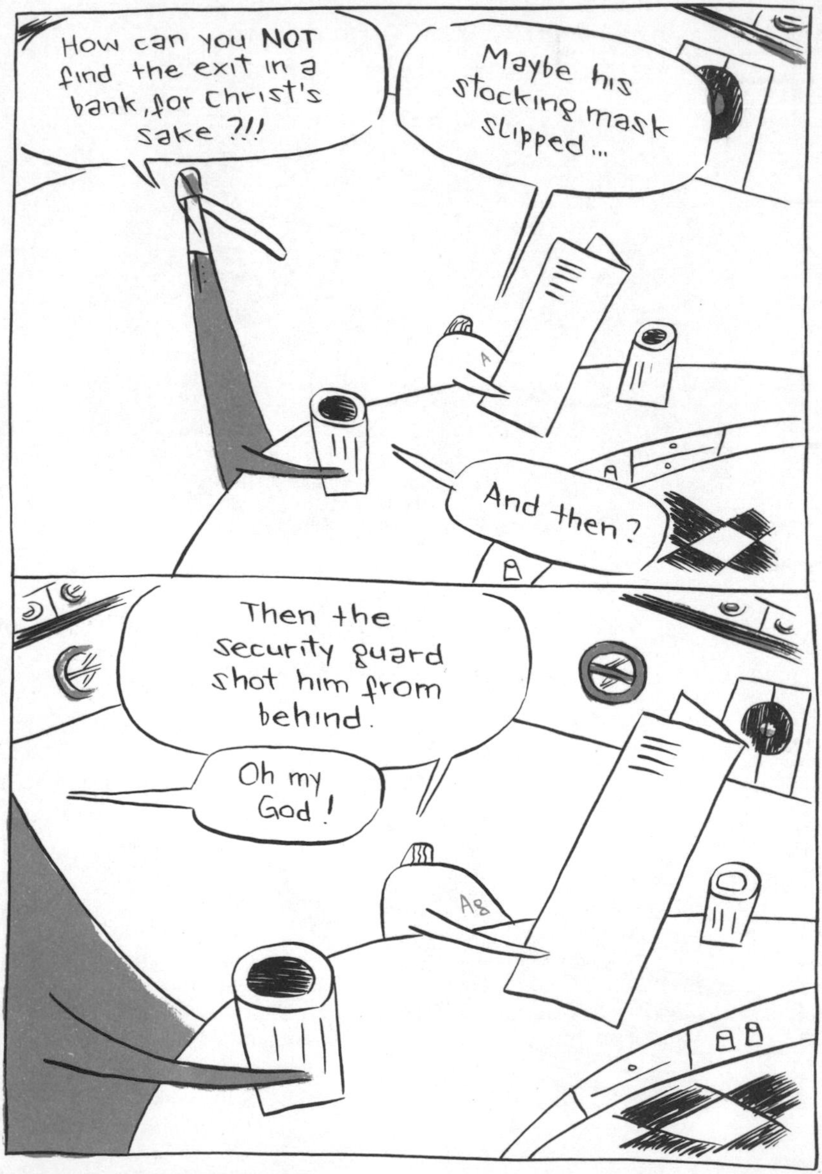
How can you NOT find the exit in a bank, for Christ's sake ?!!
Maybe his stocking mask slipped...
And then?
Then the security guard shot him from behind.
Oh my God!

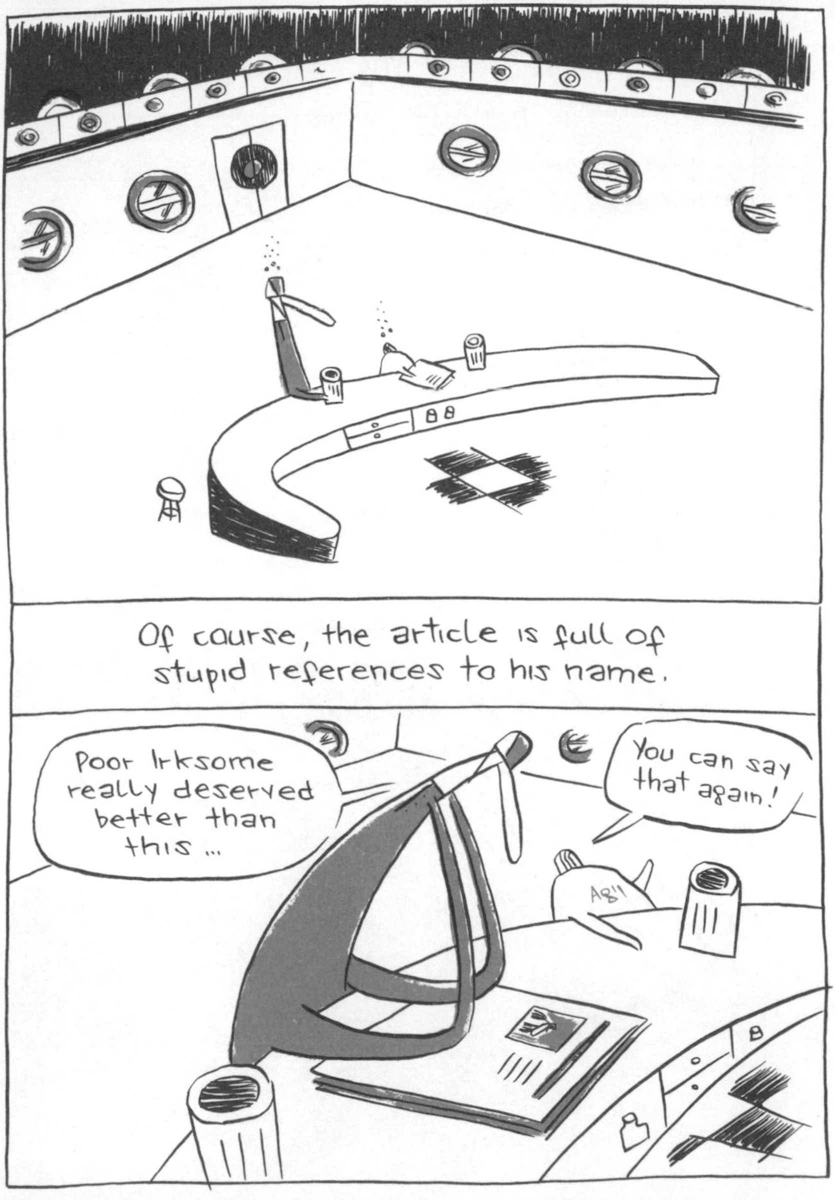
Of course, the article is full of stupid references to his name.
Poor Irksome really deserved better than this ...
You can say that again!

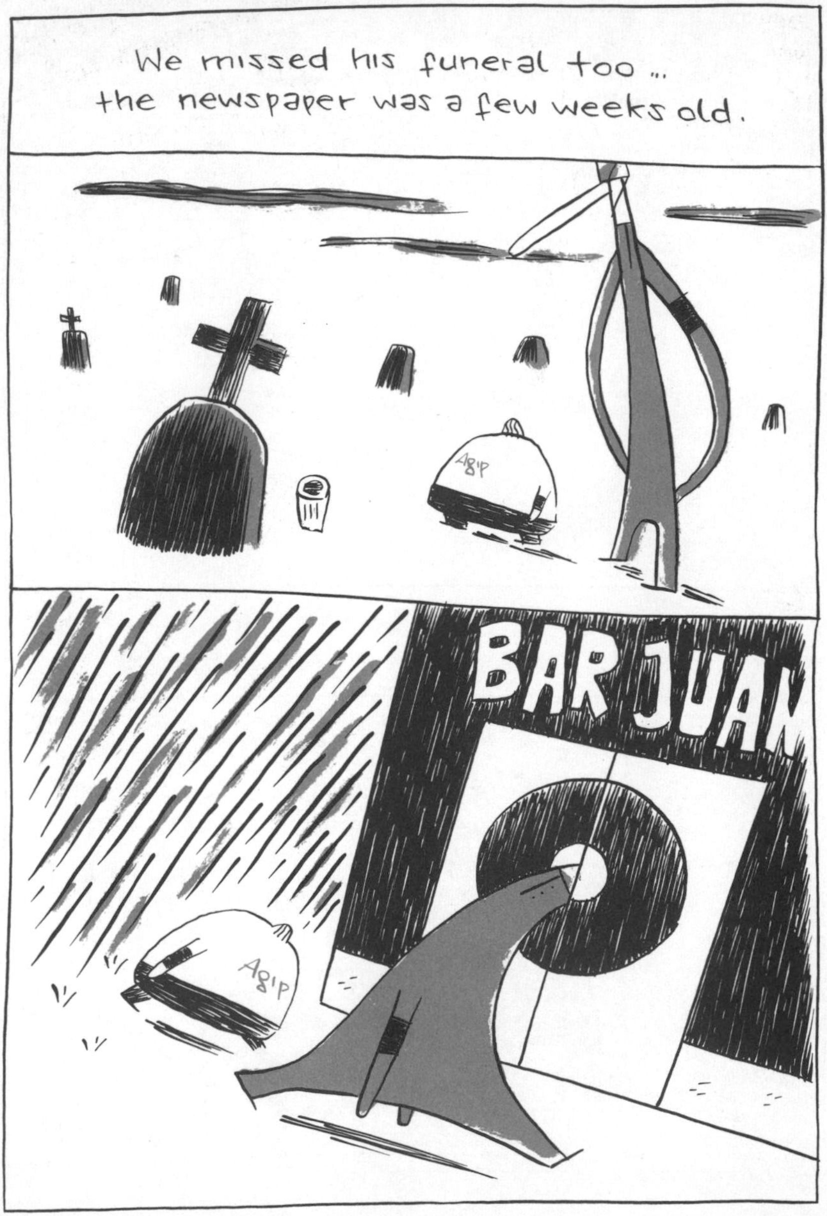
We missed his funeral too ...
the newspaper was a few weeks old.
Agip
BAR JUAN
Agip

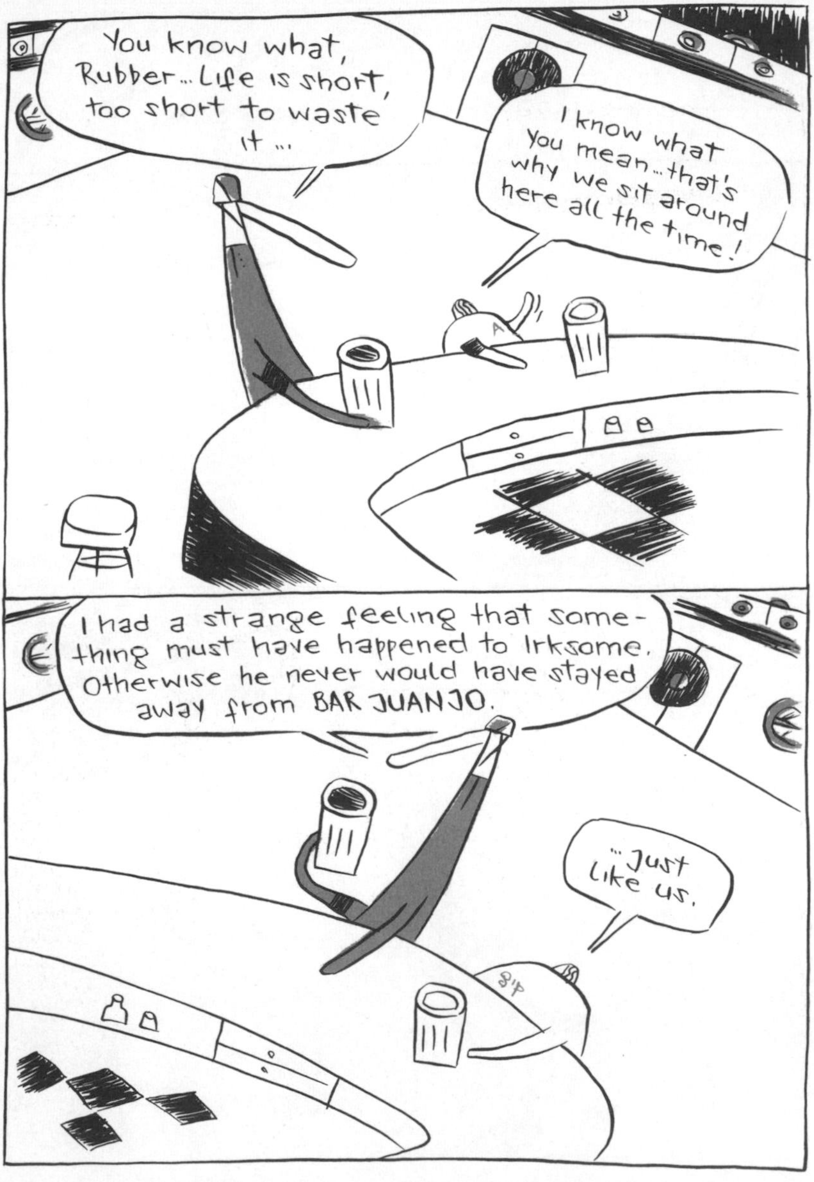
You know what, Rubber... Life is short, too short to waste it...
I know what you mean... that's why we sit around here all the time!
I had a strange feeling that something must have happened to Irksome. Otherwise he never would have stayed away from BAR JUANJO.
...Just like us.

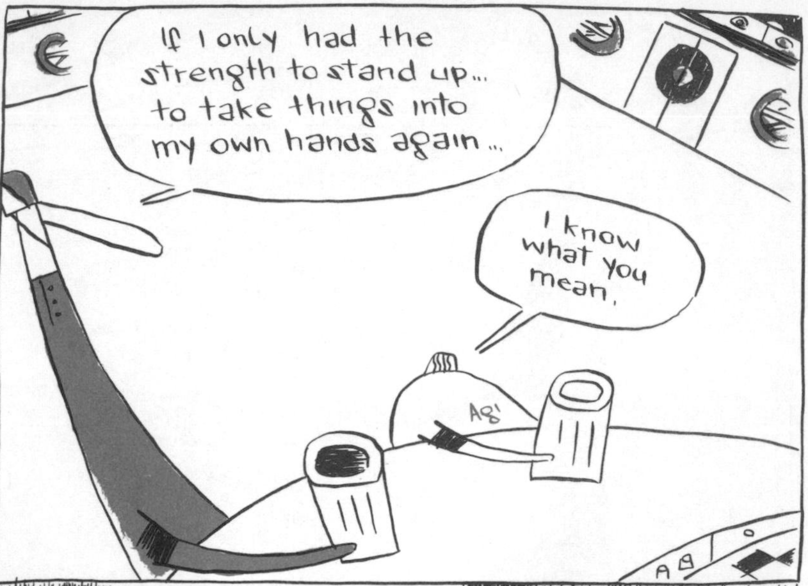
If I only had the strength to stand up... to take things into my own hands again...
I know what you mean.
Ag!
A8

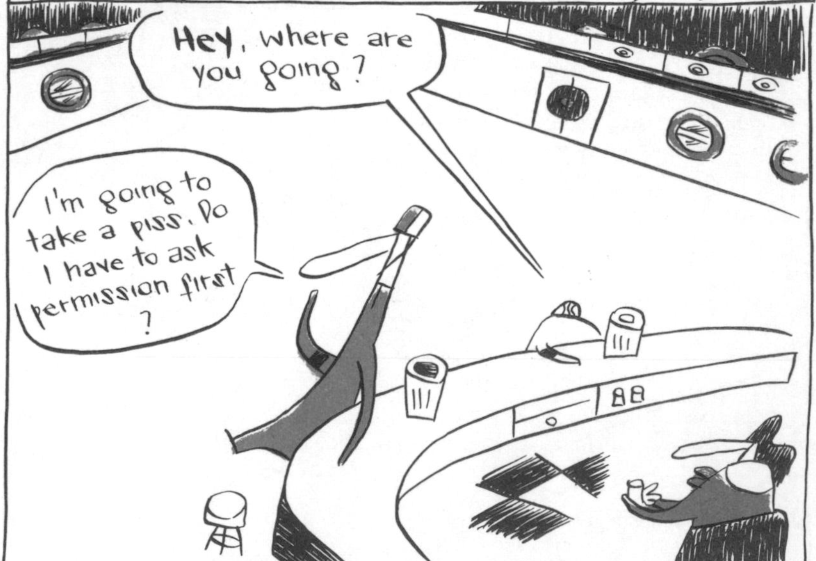
Hey, where are you going?
I'm going to take a piss. Do I have to ask permission first?
88

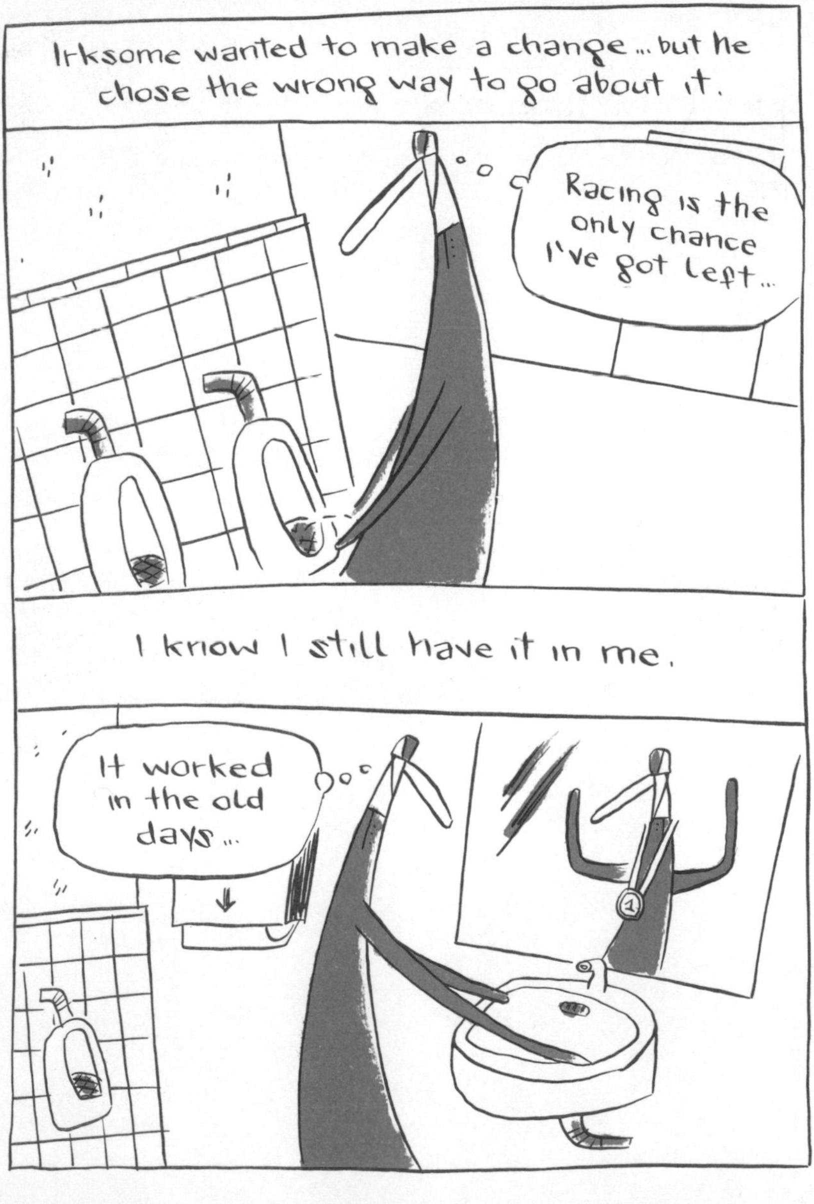
Irksome wanted to make a change... but he chose the wrong way to go about it.
Racing is the only chance I've got left...
I know I still have it in me.
It worked in the old days...

3

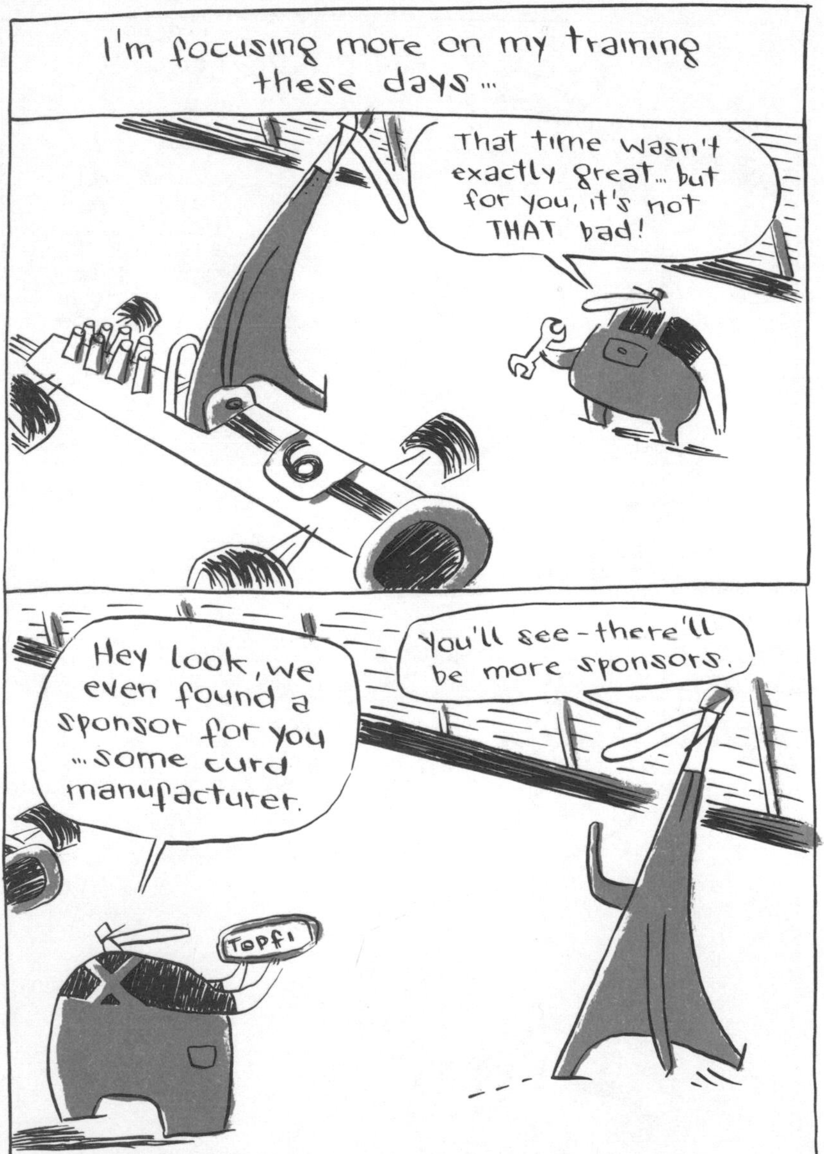
I'm focusing more on my training these days...
That time wasn't exactly great... but for you, it's not THAT bad!
Hey look, we even found a sponsor for you ...some curd manufacturer.
Topfi
You'll see - there'll be more sponsors.

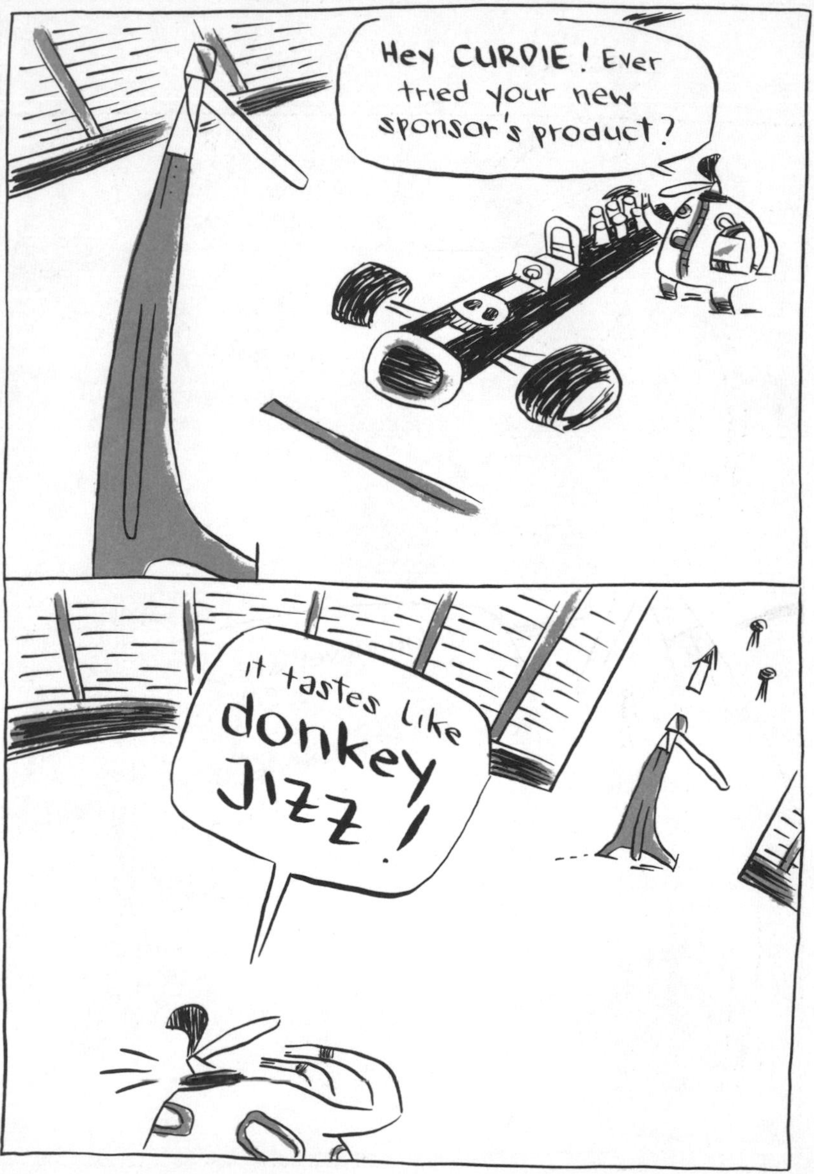
Hey CURDIE! Ever tried your new sponsor's product?
it tastes like donkey JIZZ!

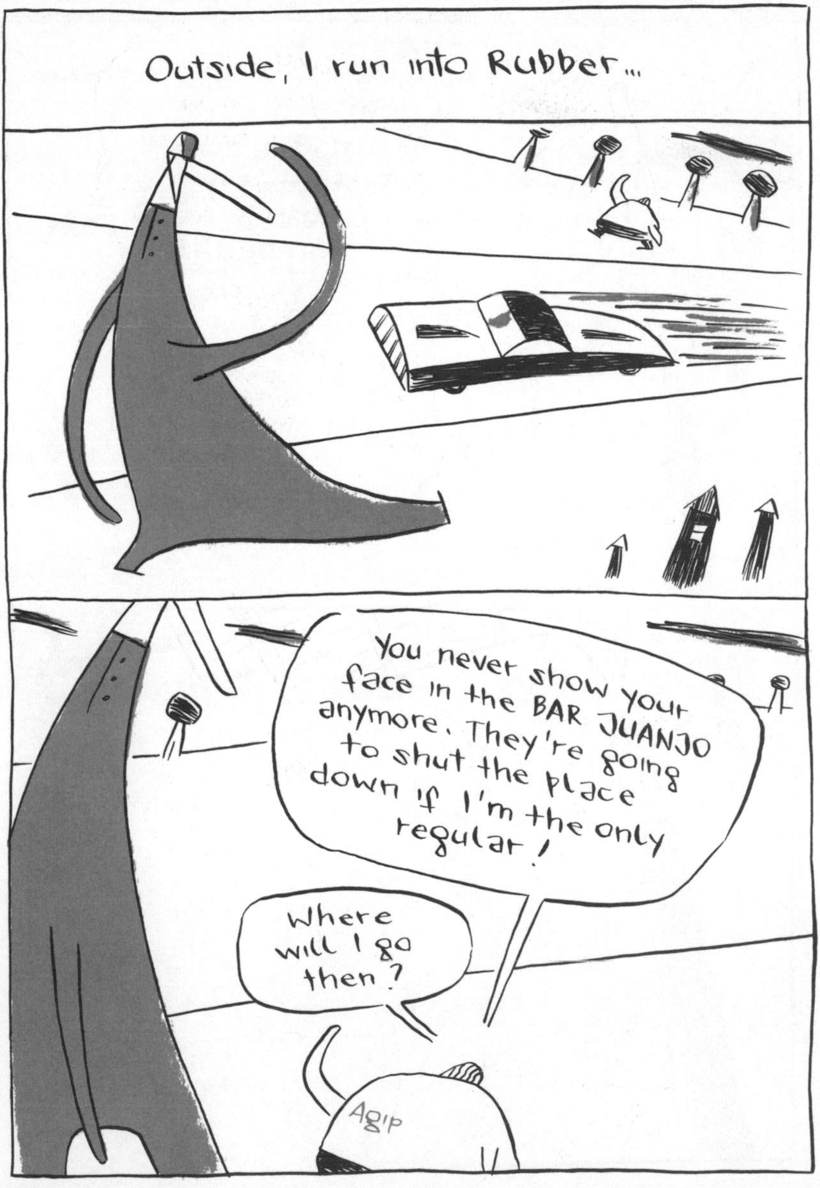
Outside, I run into Rubber...
You never show your face in the BAR JUANJO anymore. They're going to shut the place down if I'm the only regular!
Where will I go then?
Agip

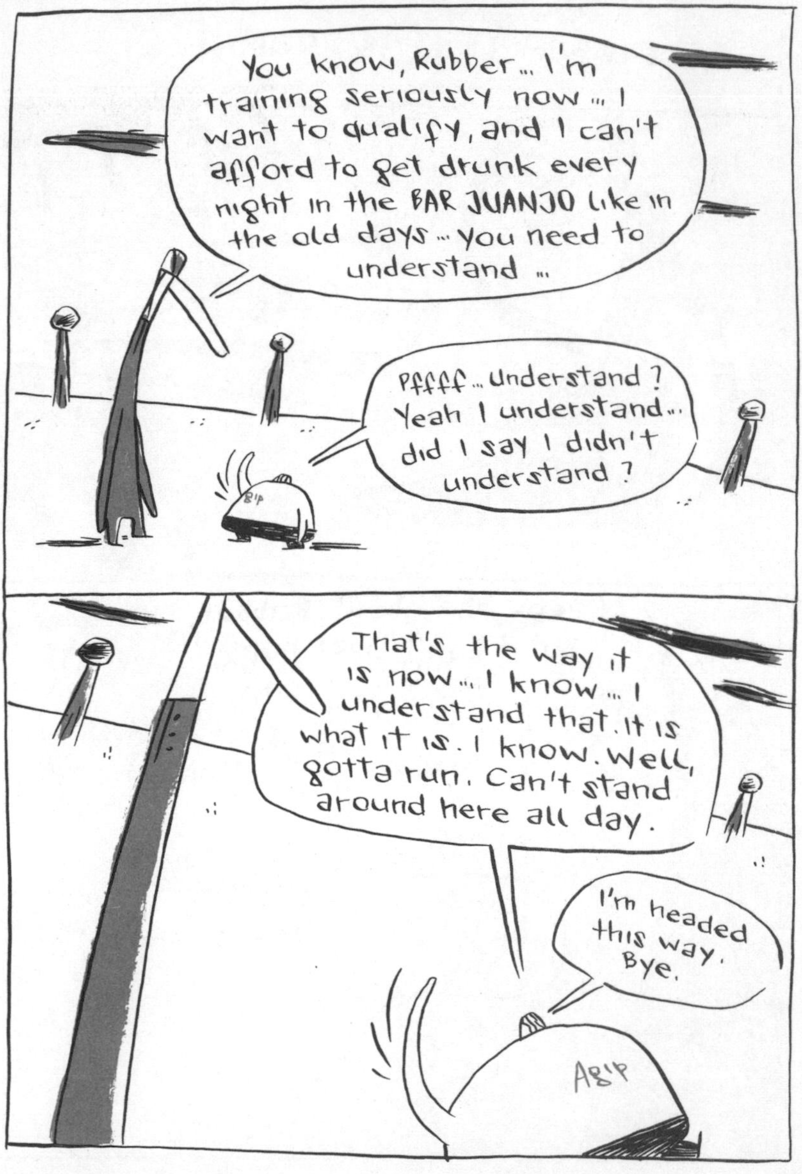
You know, Rubber... I'm training seriously now... I want to qualify, and I can't afford to get drunk every night in the BAR JUANJO like in the old days... you need to understand...
Pffff... understand? Yeah I understand... did I say I didn't understand?
Agip
That's the way it is now... I know... I understand that. It is what it is. I know. Well, gotta run. Can't stand around here all day.
I'm headed this way. Bye.
Agip

I'm sure Rubber is bored, all by himself in the BAR JUANJO every night.

I feel bad about Rubber, but I can't just hang around BAR JUANJO forever...

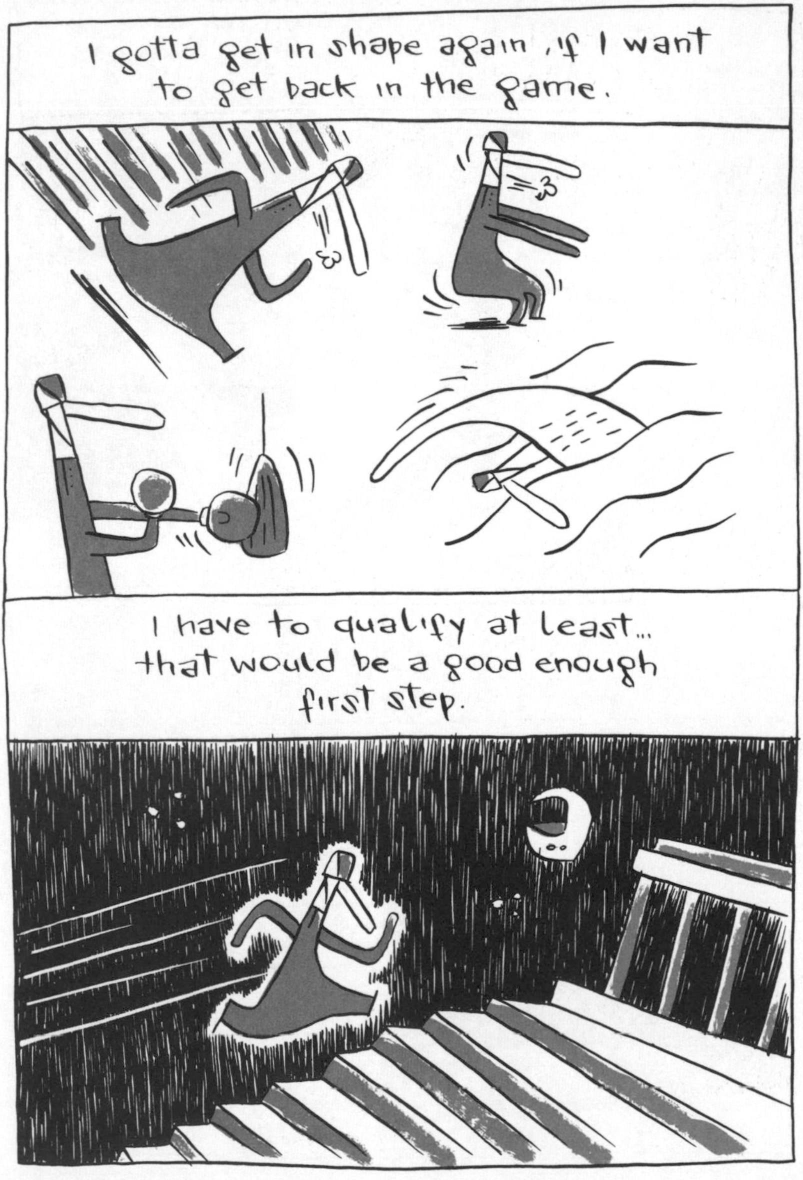
I gotta get in shape again, if I want to get back in the game.
I have to qualify at least... that would be a good enough first step.

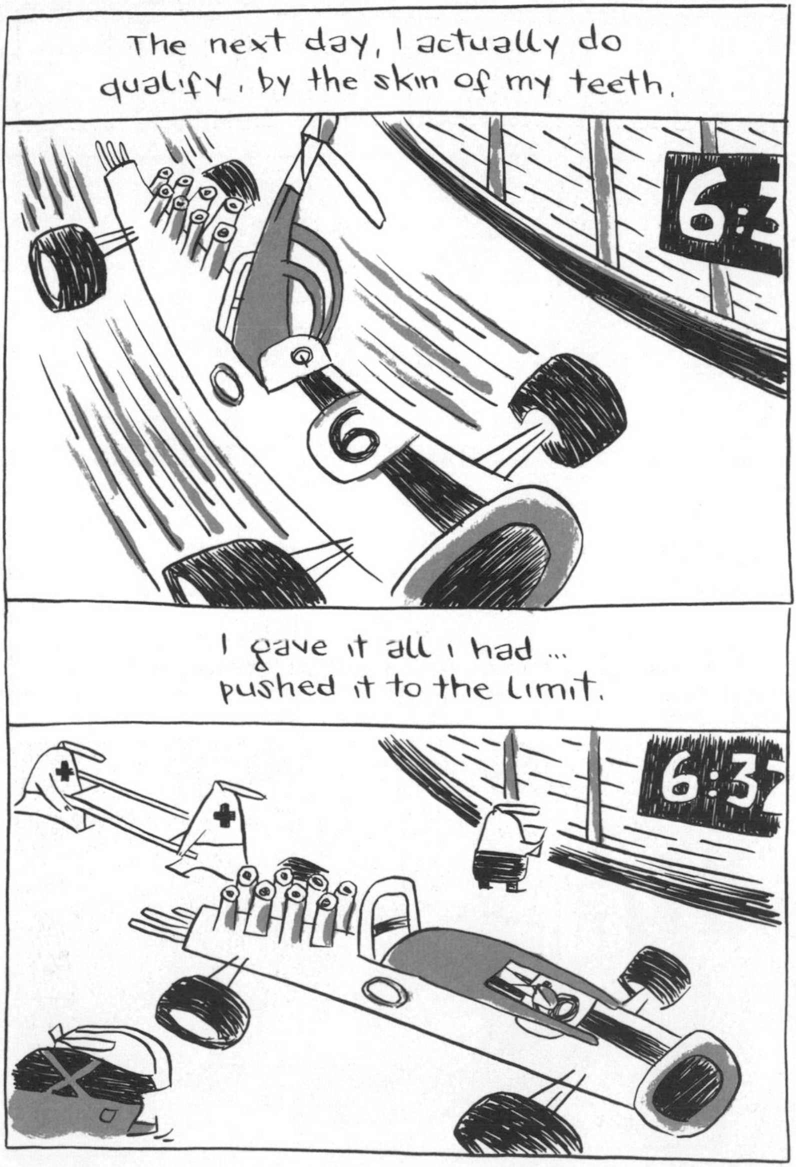
The next day, I actually do qualify, by the skin of my teeth.
I gave it all I had... pushed it to the limit.

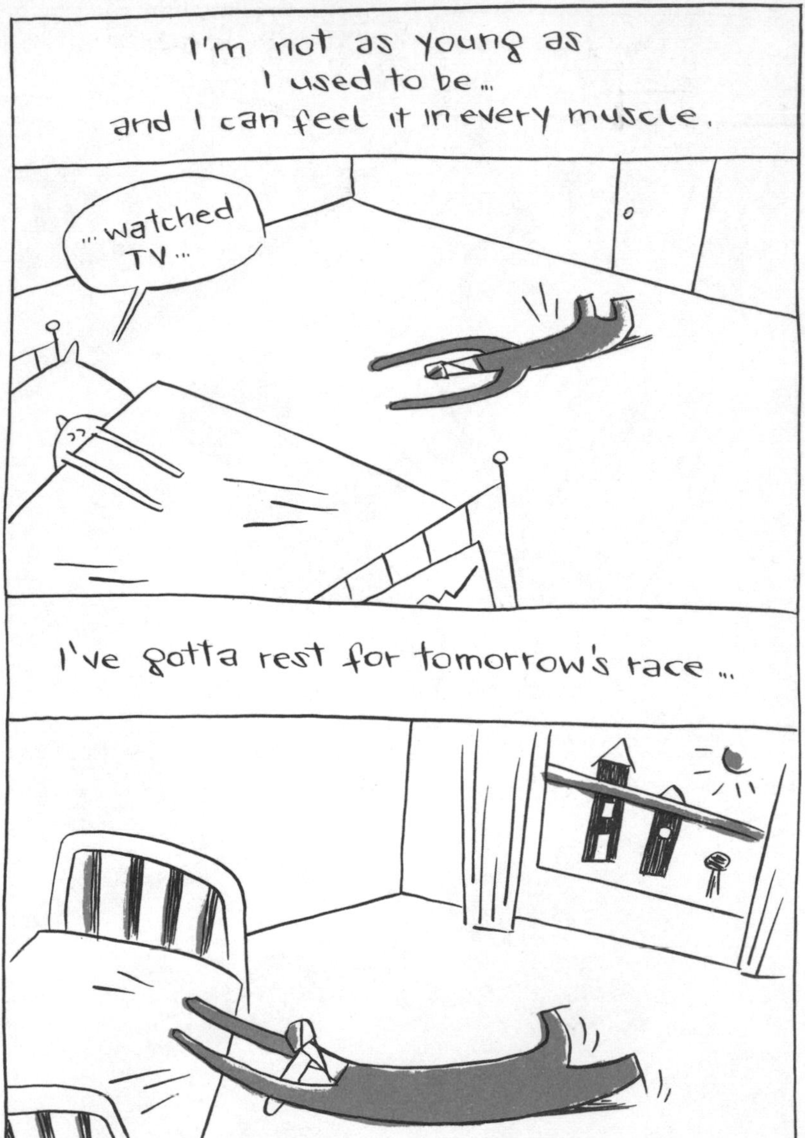
I'm not as young as I used to be... and I can feel it in every muscle.
...watched TV...
I've gotta rest for tomorrow's race...

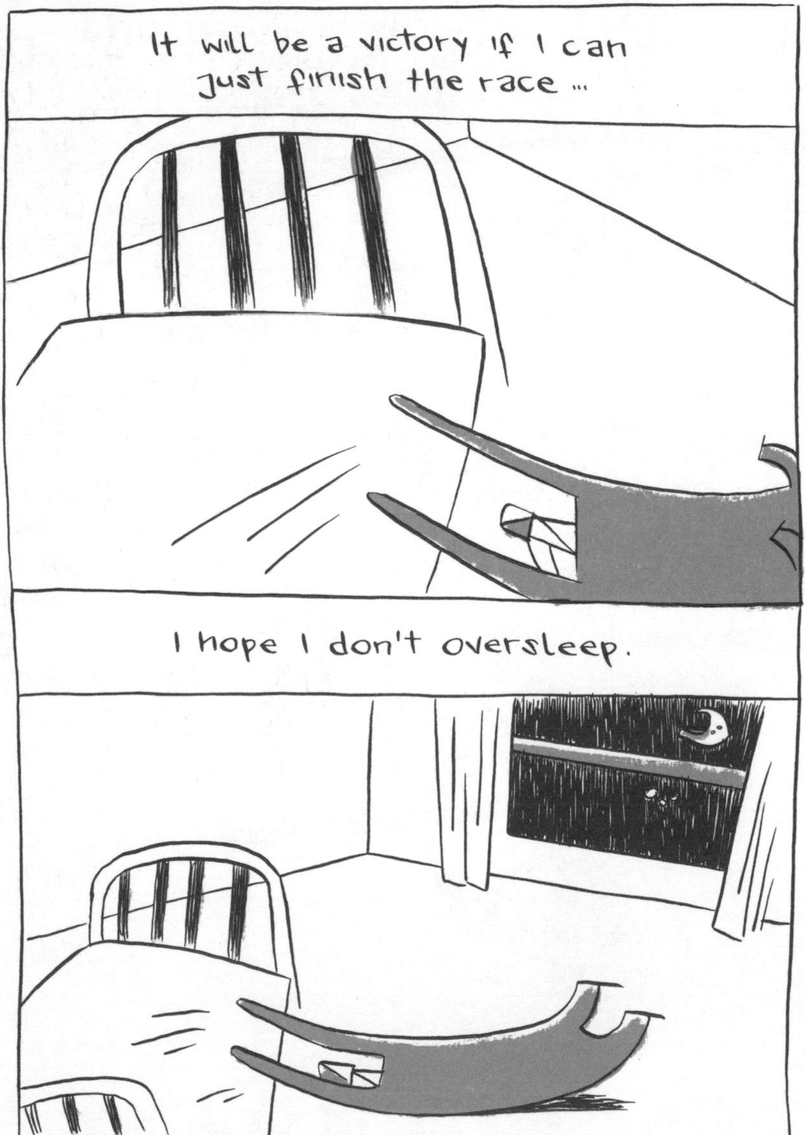
It will be a victory if I can just finish the race ...
I hope I don't oversleep.

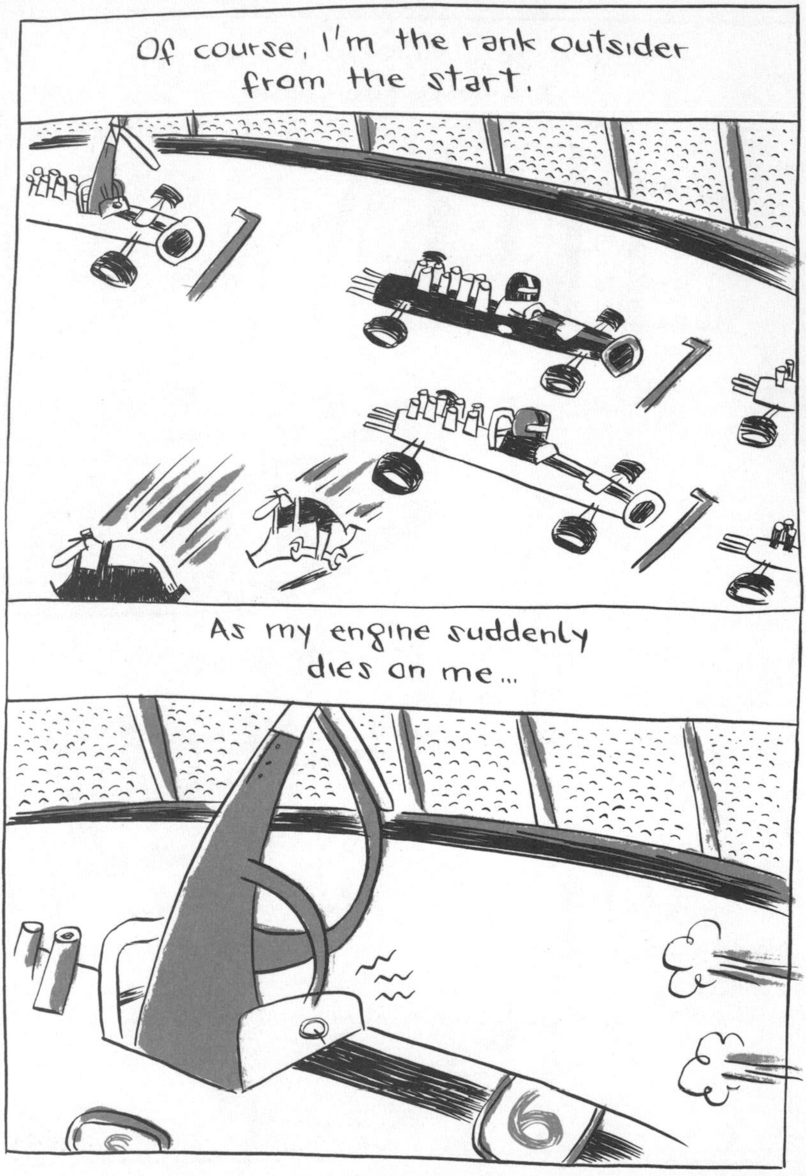
Of course, I'm the rank outsider from the start.
As my engine suddenly dies on me...

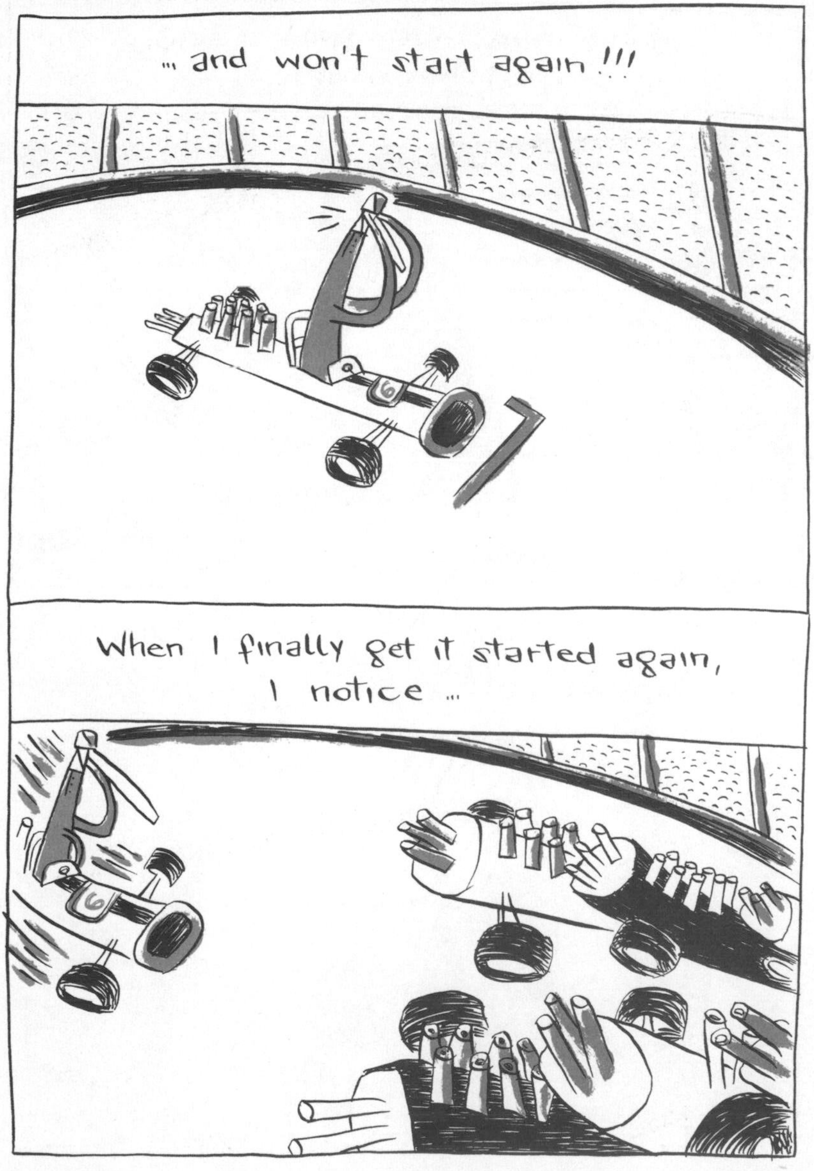
... and won't start again!!!
When I finally get it started again,
I notice ...

...there must have been a huge pile-up at the starting line!

Delli Ferolli didn't get off to a great start either. He finds himself right in front of me.

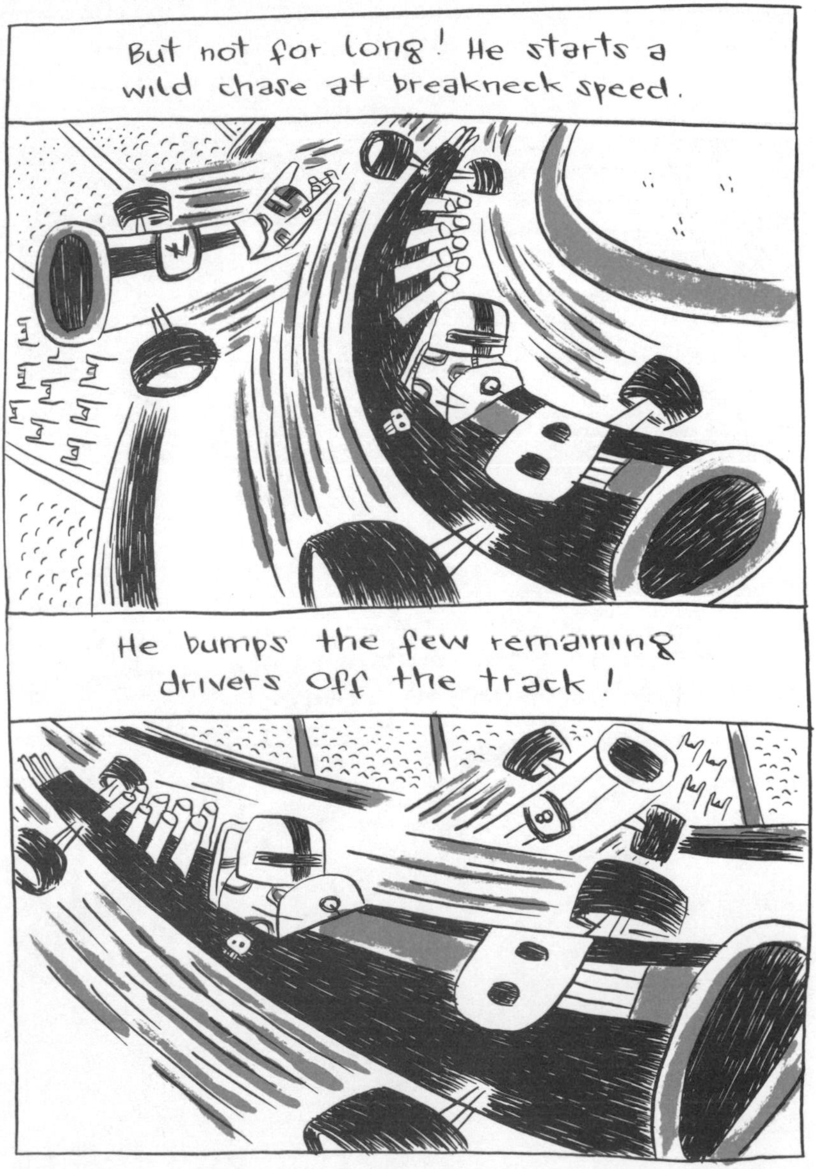
But not for long! He starts a wild chase at breakneck speed.
He bumps the few remaining drivers off the track!

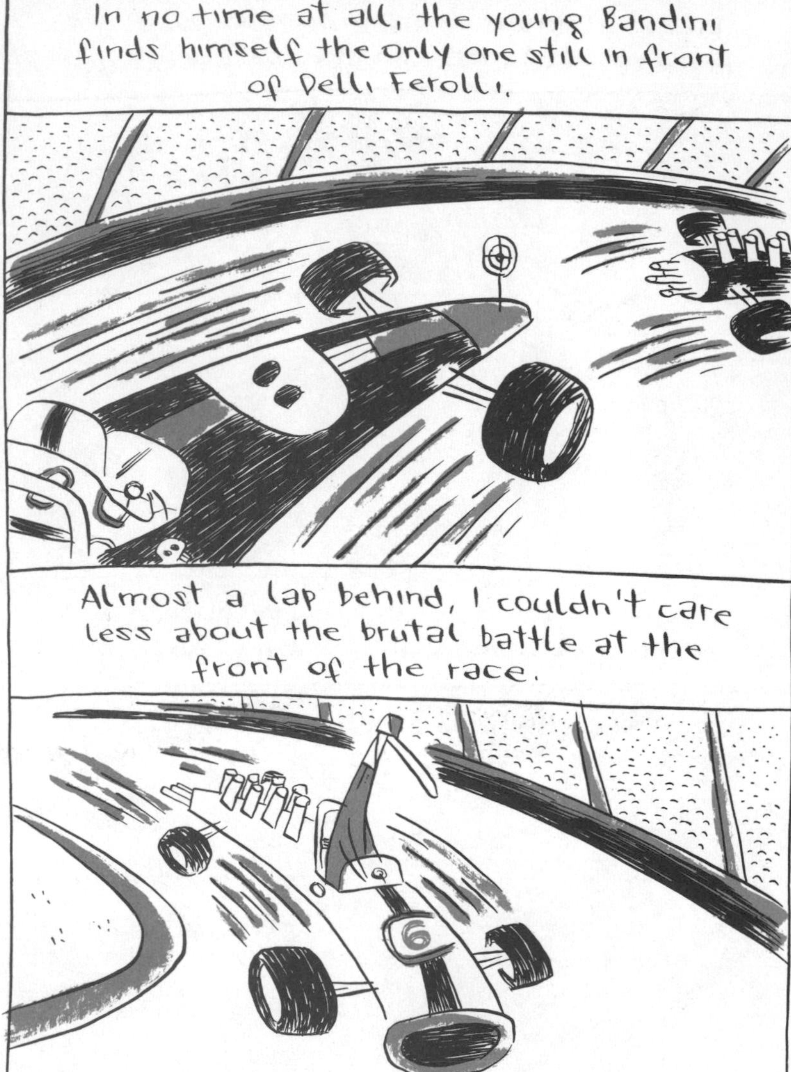
In no time at all, the young Bandini finds himself the only one still in front of Delli Ferolli.
Almost a lap behind, I couldn't care less about the brutal battle at the front of the race.
6

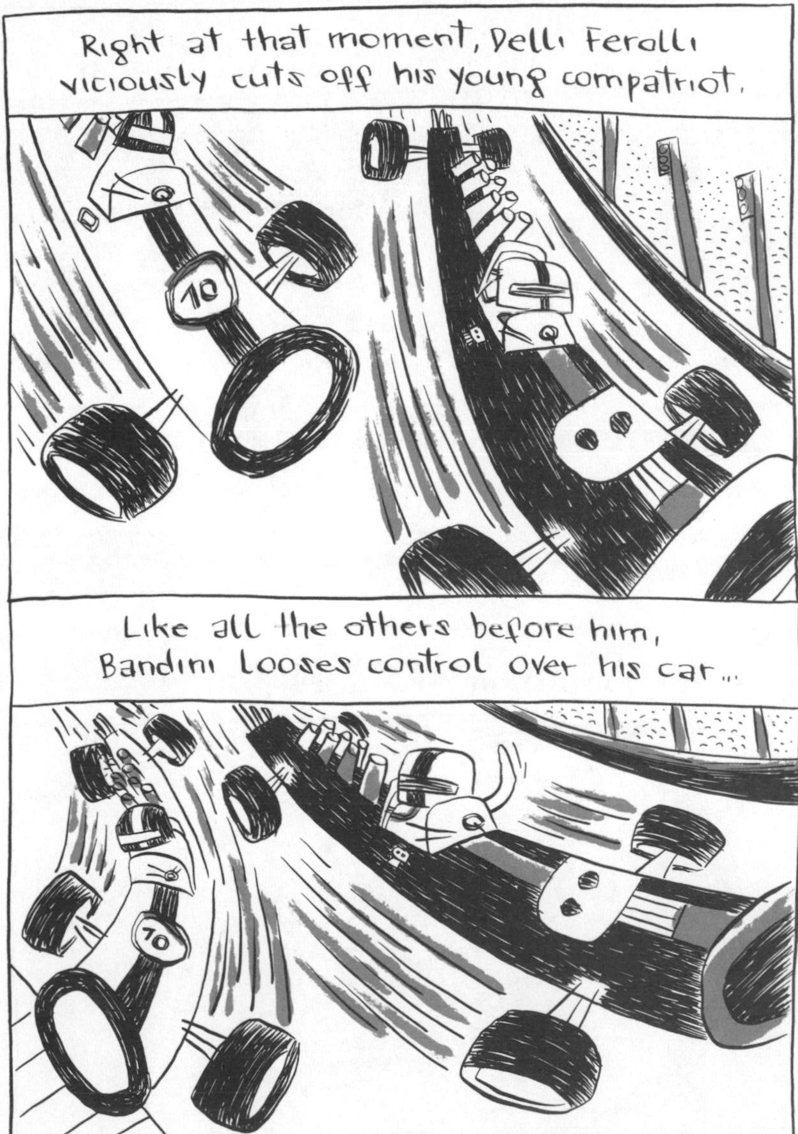
Right at that moment, Delli Ferolli viciously cuts off his young compatriot.
Like all the others before him, Bandini looses control over his car...

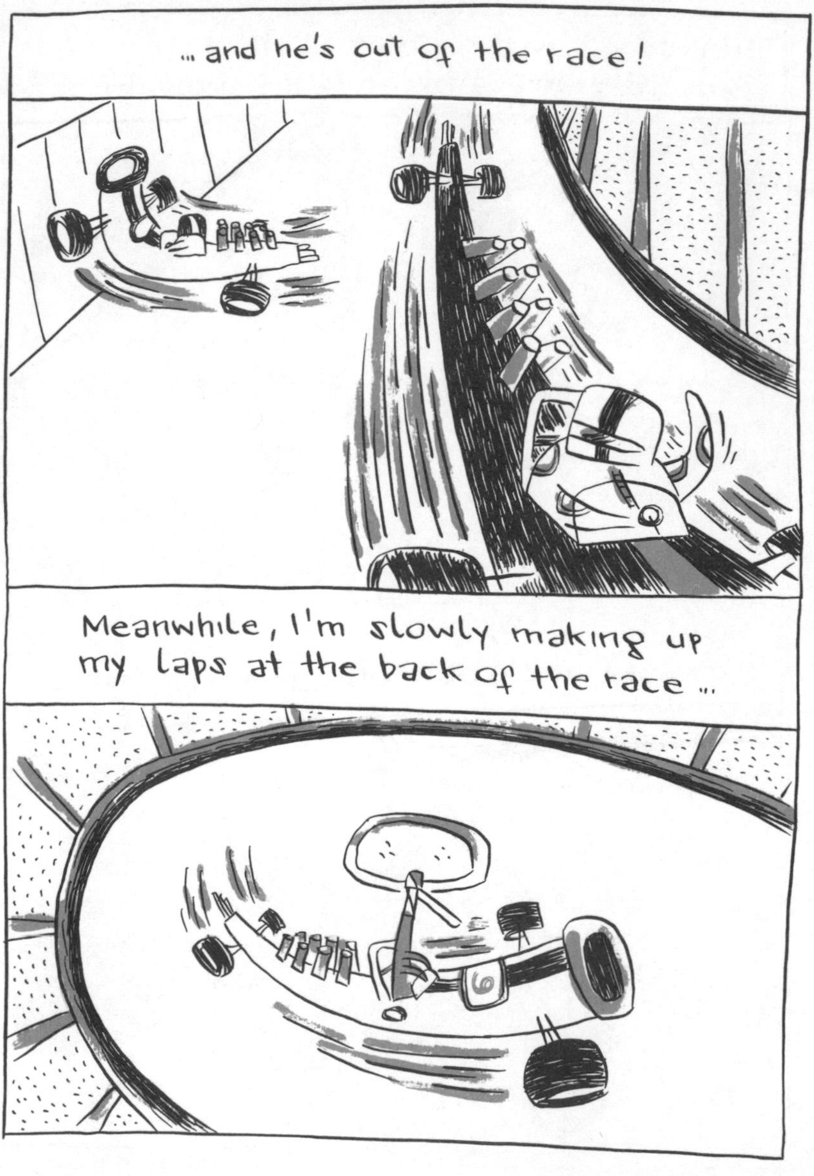
... and he's out of the race!
Meanwhile, I'm slowly making up my laps at the back of the race ...

Before I know it, here comes Delli Ferolli, looking to overtake me...

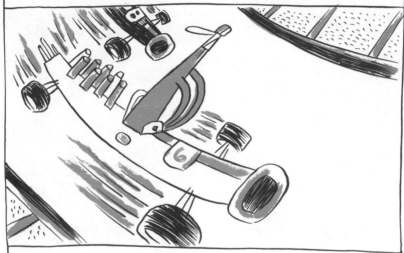

Naturally, at this point he wants to make me look old and slow.

Look Ma, no hands!

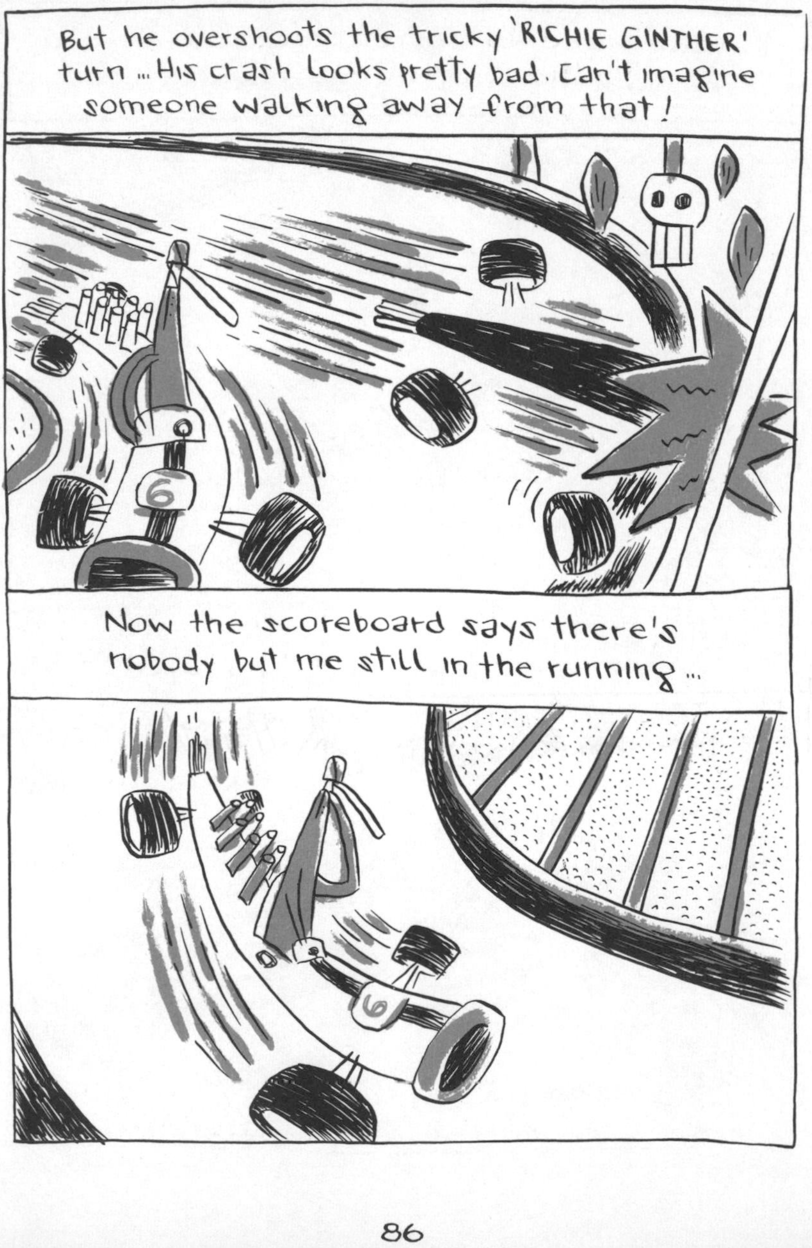
But he overshoots the tricky 'RICHIE GINTHER' turn ... His crash looks pretty bad. Can't imagine someone walking away from that!
Now the scoreboard says there's nobody but me still in the running ...
6
6

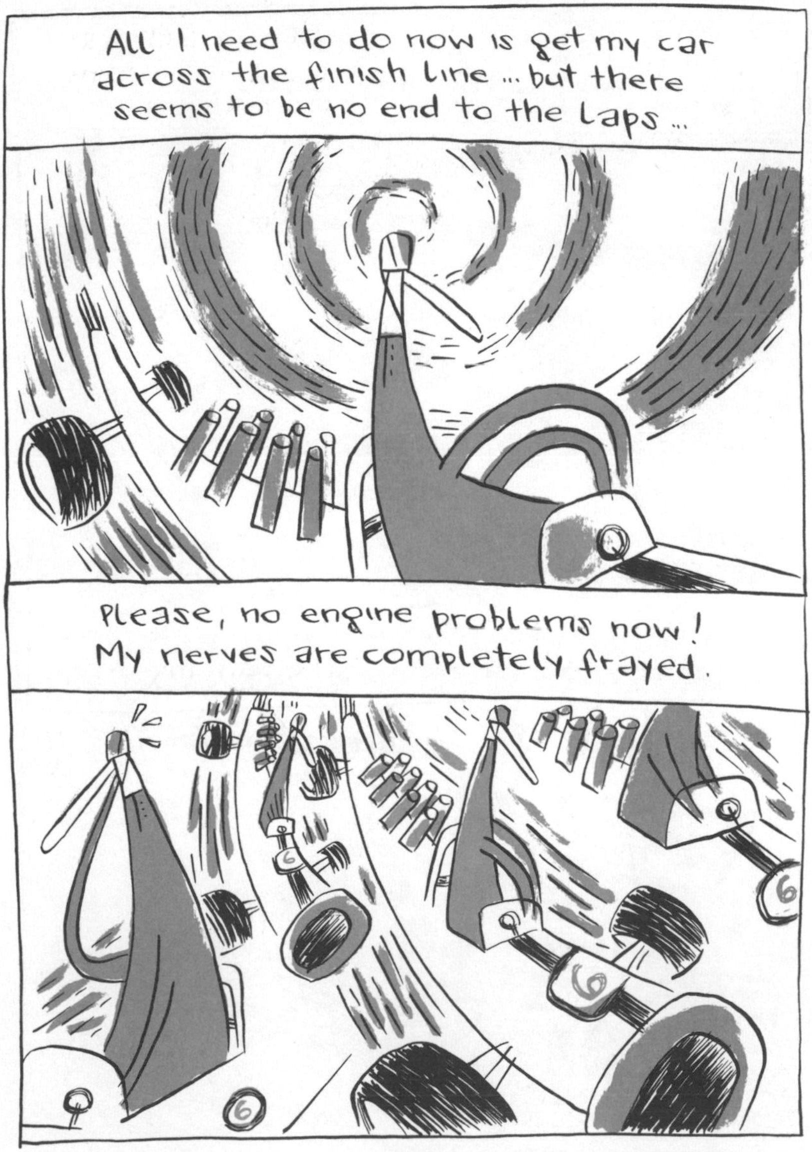
All I need to do now is get my car across the finish line ... but there seems to be no end to the laps ...
Please, no engine problems now! My nerves are completely frayed.

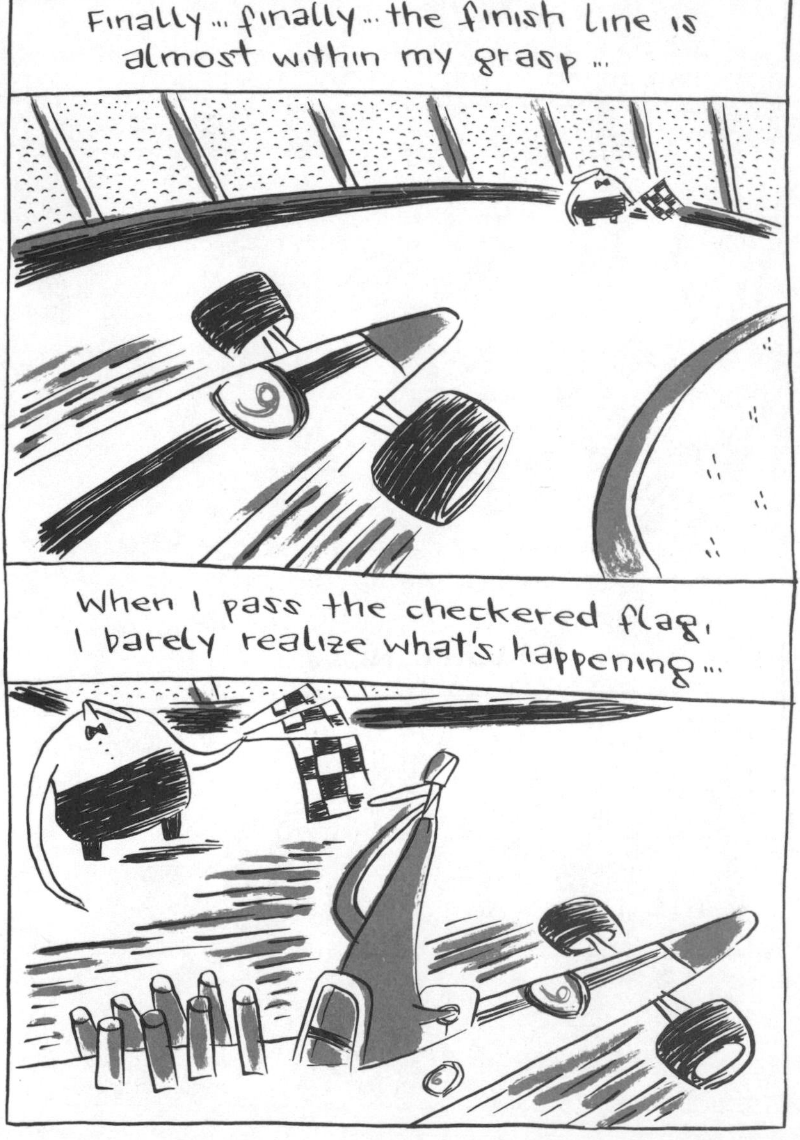
Finally... finally... the finish line is almost within my grasp...
When I pass the checkered flag, I barely realize what's happening...

In the winners' circle,
it dawns on me...

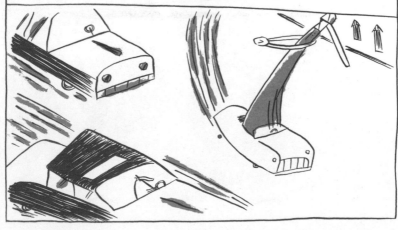

I gotta tell my wife about this
RIGHT NOW !

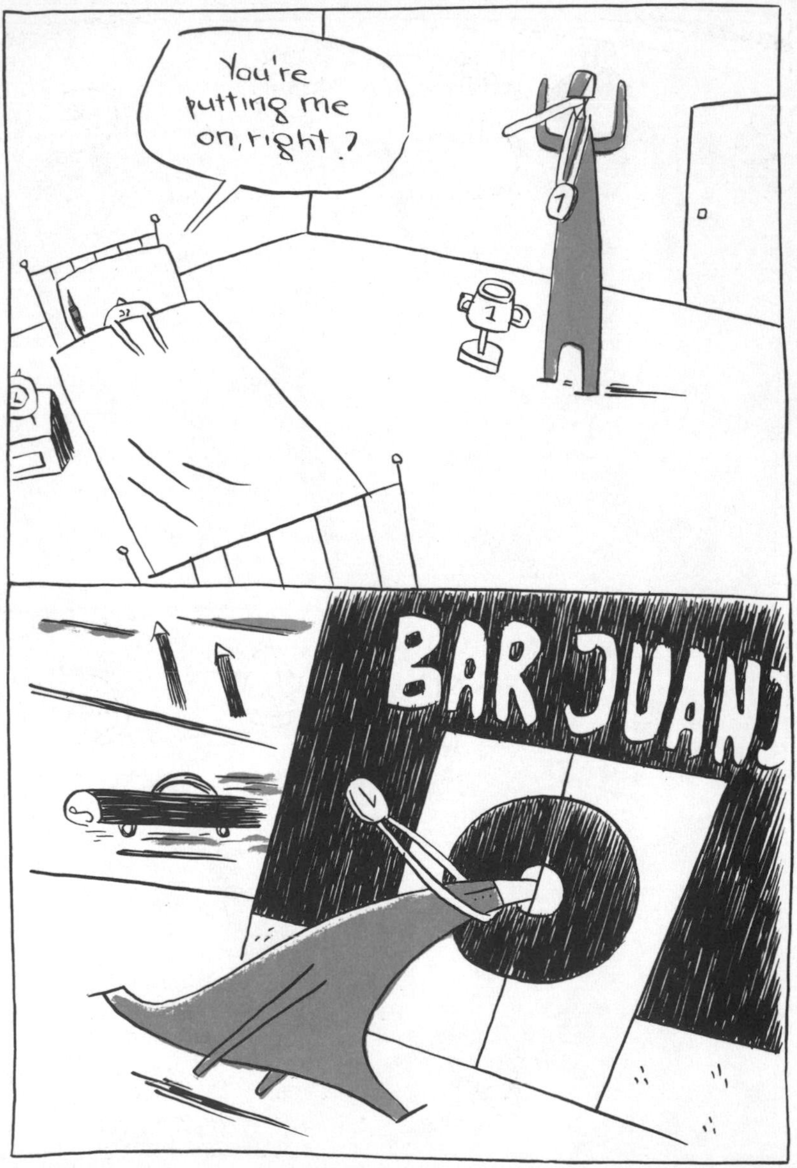
You're putting me on, right?
BAR JUAN

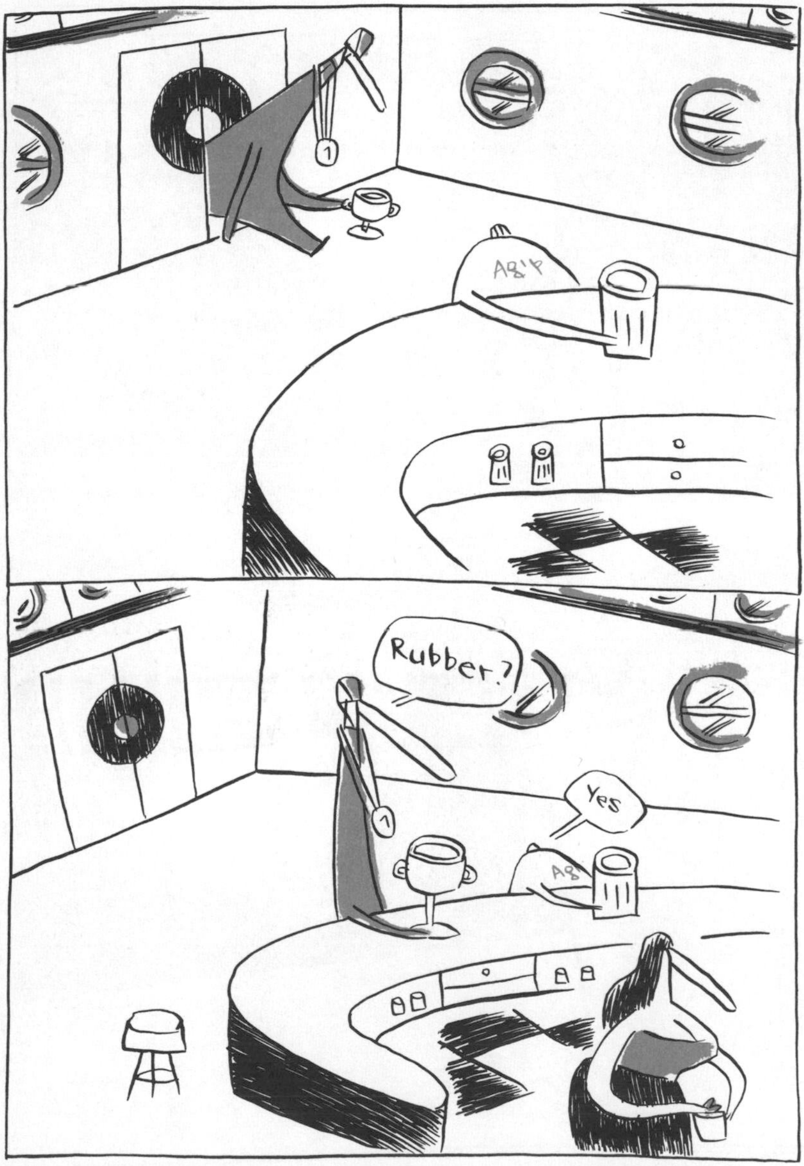
Rubber?
Yes

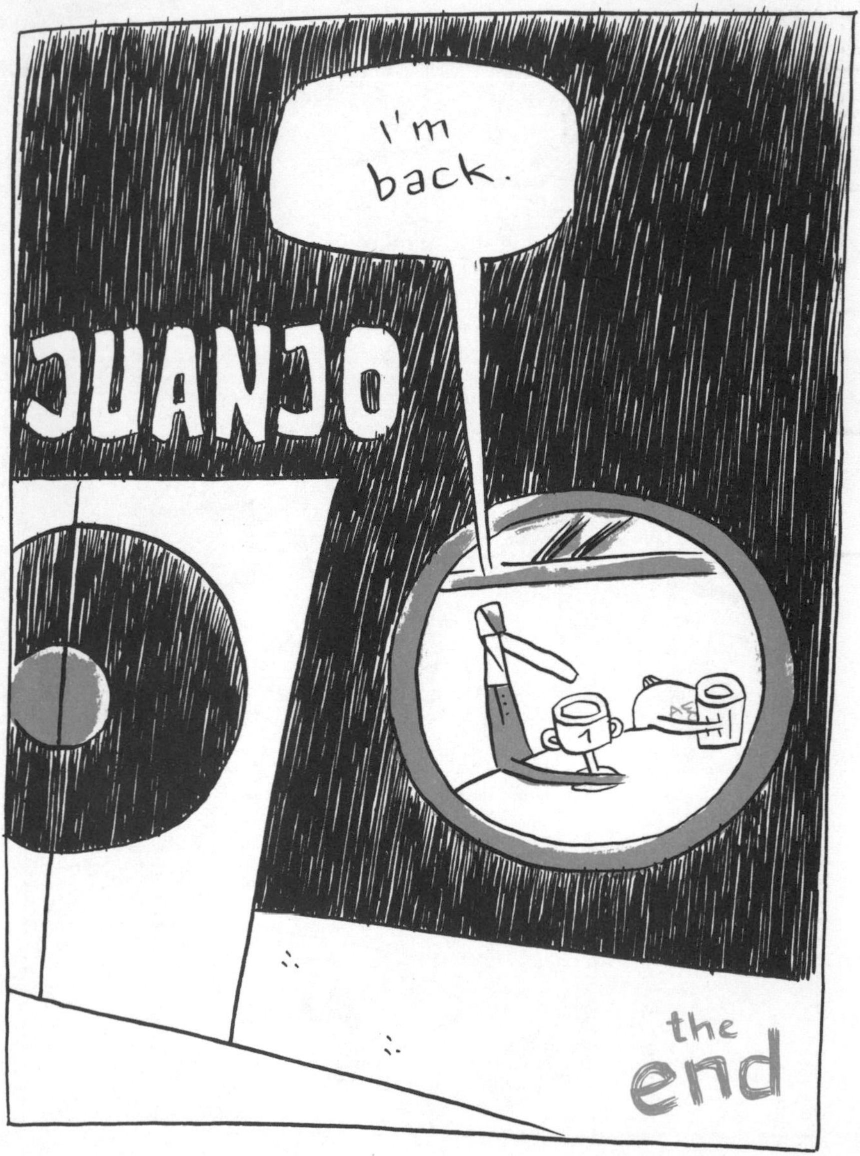
I'm back.
JUANJO
the end